Willful Acts

WILLFUL ACTS

Margaret Hollingsworth

The Coach House Press, Toronto

Copyright © 1985, Margaret Hollingsworth
Published with the assistance of the Canada Council.
These plays are fully protected by copyright.
All inquiries concerning performing rights,
professional or amateur, readings, or any other
use of this material should be directed to:
Margaret Hollingsworth
c/o Playwrights Union of Canada
8 York Street, 6th floor
Toronto, Ontario M5J 1R2

Cover design: Gordon Robertson
Text design: Nelson Adams
Editor for the Press: Robert Wallace
Author photo: Allan Hymers
The Coach House Press
401 (rear) Huron Street
Toronto, Canada M5S 2G5

Canadian Cataloguing in Publication Data
Hollingsworth, Margaret, 1939-
Willful acts
ISBN 0-88910-304-6
I. Title.
PS 8565.054 W 54 1985   C 812'.54   C 85-098621-4
PR 9199.3.H 65 W 54 1985

Contents

for Allan

Introduction

Willful Acts is about women and their relationships. In these five plays Margaret Hollingsworth presents woman exploring, projecting, provoking, and sometimes escaping from the need to come to terms with herself and her environment. Neither peripheral nor passive, she is yet aware that while she observes others, she herself is not always noted, and until she acts, she will not be seen or heard. Like the heroine of 'Widecombe Fair,' one of Hollingsworth's recent short stories, she has been granted full rights of citizenship but remains an English-speaking alien.[1] And from this isolated point of view she must carve out both a space and a language in order to build her world.

Sometimes that point of view is split between the external, ostensibly 'real' world in which a role is imposed upon her, and the – to her – truer reality from which she looks out: Gemma, in *The Apple in the Eye*, for example, recognizes all too clearly the distinction between her husband Martin's ordered, reductive, factually objective universe and her own expansive, encircling, imaginative inner life, and actually watches herself deftly weave the one through the other. In *Islands*, on the other hand, both Alli and Muriel deliberately reject that outerworld, refusing to cope with it on any level: Alli elects madness where, her mind in 'cold storage,' she does not have to apologize for her actions and words because she is 'sick' and so can move freely, untouched, through the lives of others, while Muriel retires into isolation, seeking a self-sufficiency where she runs no risk of hurting others, or herself.

Sometimes the imaginative innerworld is surrealistically imposed on the framework of the outer life, as in *Diving*, where Viveca can safely compose the male/female, mother/daughter relationships into new metaphorical patterns. At other times the external structure is wilfully destroyed in order to achieve the

9

inner dream, just as Luce fends off Chuck in *Ever Loving* to create her own independent life in the new world; but the obverse too is, threateningly, always there, and in the same play the other two war brides, Ruth and Diana, find their hopes and plans overwhelmed and submerged in the strange, new and demanding environments of their husbands.

And sometimes, as in *War Babies*, that innerworld becomes a mirror, reflecting the pain and oppressiveness of separation and the constant struggle to bridge two isolations: 'I thought I'd try to put you in my position, so you'd really know how it feels,' Esme explains as she writes a play about her life with Colin from the other side of the looking glass.

But always, in all of Margaret Hollingsworth's plays, it is this mental landscape one notices first, and then the need for a relationship with it, the need in fact to feel at home. 'Home comes in again and again in my work,' Hollingsworth admits. 'It's about relating to the place that you're in and finding a place for yourself in a foreign environment....'[2] 'Home meant limits, security, love – a barrier against the outside,' muses the heroine of 'Widecombe Fair'; 'Home meant familiarity....'

Home also means sharing, talking to each other, above all, listening. 'I get the feeling you two should talk more,' the nurse Paddy tells Colin in *War Babies*. 'We talk all the time,' protests Colin. 'Real talk,' replies Paddy. And so they do talk all the time – to themselves, to each other, to the audience. Hollingsworth's characters are fluent to the limit of endurance, pushing words, images, ideas to the wall in their effort to be heard and felt. For 'real talk' requires not only listening but emotional engagement. 'Words. But where are the feelings?' asks Esme. Where, also, are the right questions? 'They're walking around you know. All over town,' Alli confides to Rose. 'Questions.' Words, feelings, questions, listening – all must be managed into a pattern of familiarity before one can feel safe. And so these plays are ultimately about bridge-building through narration, relating actively in an equation of responsibility. 'How to make you hear when you do not know how to listen,' Luce cries out to Chuck. When nobody listens, no one notices, and the equation splinters, leaving the characters to face a limitless void. 'We're always trying to contain ... look for limits,' playwright Esme has her creation Colin 2 say. 'Without limits we go mad, don't we?'

It is on the brink of this precipice that most of Hollingsworth's characters live. Indeed, the most realistic play in this volume, *Islands*, takes characters from an even earlier stage life, *Alli Alli Oh* (1977),[3] and pushes them over the edge. At the end of that earlier one-act play, Alli escapes into madness in order to run away from a relationship that has gone nerve-rendingly wrong, leaving Muriel to deal with a calving cow and a farm she cannot manage on her own. Now, six months later, in *Islands*, Muriel has achieved an uneasy truce with her environment, but the stage directions, in describing a setting that is only 'roughly finished,' reflect the tenuousness of her new-found stability. Only 'roughly finished,' the house has been professionally wired, but the insulation is incomplete; the blueprints for a new dwelling are drawn up, but the drawing table is still in pieces and the screen door needs new hinges. Centering has taken place at the expense of relationships and the threat of her mother's conservative, conventional, male-oriented universe, followed almost immediately by the demands of Alli's return, is more than Muriel can face. In the end some things are accomplished: Alli's uninhibited frankness serves as a catalyst towards honesty, and Rose must confront the fact of her daughter's lesbianism; Alli herself knows, because she has listened to the environment, that her return was a mistake even before she enters the house; Muriel has the strength to reject the emotional demands of both mother and former lover. But the calm of the play's conclusion is not completely reassuring, and we suspect that no man – or woman – can be an island.

Alli Alli Oh and its companion piece *Islands* are both

set on an island off the west coast of British Columbia, an environment Margaret Hollingsworth herself enjoyed for some years and repeatedly returns to. Another early play, whose absence from this volume I regret, is her first two-act play, *Mother Country*,[4] which also has a west-coast setting, and where the themes of home and belonging are set in a larger context still of culture and country. *Ever Loving*, which received its first production the same year (but at the other end of the country) as *Mother Country*, further explores the problems of belonging, through the lives of three immigrants thrown up by the tide of war. In this play there is a marked advance in formal experiment. Time as well as space is fluid in *Ever Loving*; voices are orchestrated, fantasies wind through and about moments of heightened realism, accent plays against the idioms of different Canadian regions, silence acts upon silence, moments of deep personal significance parallel the pettiness of domestic confrontation, all woven together by musical interludes which, with the insistence on period costume, deftly place the events in historical perspective. This is a musical play with a difference – the songs are hauntingly familiar, comfortably redolent of time and place, while the events of the three women's lives are individual, painful in their intimate revelations, perceptive in their unveiling of three different bewilderments as English Diana, Scottish Ruthie and Italian Luce struggle to come to terms with environments not of their own making or conscious choosing. *Ever Loving* has frequently been compared to John Murrell's *Waiting for the Parade*, but whereas the latter play portrays with unflinching realism the lives of women left at home during the war, Hollingsworth's *Ever Loving*, through a variety of modes, explores the fate of those who must make a new home in a strange unfamiliar culture.

Hollingsworth's work for the theatre ranges from full-length plays with conventional stage settings and large casts to miniatures with one, two or three characters; from comedies of situation and character to

fantasy voyages through strange mental landscapes.
Two early plays are unfortunately not represented in
this collection. In *Bushed,* two retired immigrant
workers meet each day in the laundromat and against
the rhythm of sheet-folding, humming machines and
ceaseless mimed action of housewives, weave their own
fantasies, dream their own dreams. *Operators,* like
Bushed, is set in northern Ontario (the region
Hollingsworth first settled in after emigrating from
England); like *Bushed,* it reflects the innerworlds of
workers – this time two women on factory night shift –
as they try to build a friendship without communicating
the facts of their daily lives.[5] In this collection, *The Apple
in the Eye* and *Diving* pursue this more lyrical, abstract
aspect of Hollingsworth's work, reflecting her long
training in writing for radio and her keen ear for
nuances of speech and both regional and cultural
differences. In all her work she accurately captures
fluctuations in tone, tempo and accent; in these two
plays she pursues these delicate distinctions even
further by giving us multiple voices which still
unerringly belong to the one personality. Internal
monologue, actual conversations, stream of
consciousness and verbal imagery dance balletically
through her protagonist's mind, swaying back and
forward in time and space, playing with words and
images, proffering a sensibility that cries out to be
heard, seen, understood on every level.

Wordplay and multiple focus are carried further still
in the most recent play published here, *War Babies.*
Again our responses are orchestrated – sometimes
('Pause') we are allowed to think, other times ('Beat') not.
Again the protagonist goes on a journey through time,
space and personality. But this time her vehicles are a
typewriter and an unborn baby, and the scope has been
broadened to incorporate not only the familiar themes
of listening, relationships, home and culture, but the
nurturing of art, life and peace. 'War games. We play war
games. It helps keep the balance of power,' Esme
assures an astonished Paddy of the deadly accurate,

wickedly witty repartee she and Colin indulge in. How does one define creativity and use it for peace, not war? What is the difference between fact and fantasy? What shapes newspaper and television reportage? What is the difference between journalism and playwriting? What should the theatre do, what can it do? When (and where) is truth? All these questions are pursued by Esme as she creates her play within a play using the real people around her, trying to force her sense of family into unfamiliar poses for clearer focus. And all these questions, including the art of the playwright herself, are explored by Hollingsworth (who has also been a journalist) as she examines not only the place of war in art, but the place of art in our culture.

All of these plays cry out to be acted; each one provides superb roles for performers and striking challenges for directors who are not content to take the easy way out. Hollingsworth's long career in the theatre (she received her first playwriting award while still in England before she was twenty-one and her radio plays have been broadcast not only in Canada and Britain, but Australia, New Zealand and West Germany) has earned her the freedom and experience to experiment with staging, characterization, and technical effects with a sureness and skill that are reflected in her work for both stage and radio. Her own experience as an immigrant and her briefer sojourns working in Italy and Japan have endowed her with a sensitivity and empathy evident in her approach to place and person and a sense of perspective that relatively few contemporary Canadian playwrights enjoy. While written with stylishness and wit from a woman's point of view, these plays are not rigidly feminist; although rooted in place, they are not restrictively regional. They speak both of Canada and the human condition. Above all, they present a welcome, unique voice in Canadian theatre; they are indeed *Willful Acts*.

Anne Saddlemyer
Graduate Centre for Study of Drama
University of Toronto

Introduction

Notes

1 'Widecombe Fair,' *Room of One's Own*, vol. 9, no. 3 (August 1984), pp. 44-57.

2 Interview in *The Work: Conversations with English-Canadian Playwrights*, ed. Robert Wallace and Cynthia Zimmerman (Toronto: Coach House Press, 1982), pp. 91-101.

3 *Alli Alli Oh* (Toronto: Playwrights Co-op, 1979), first produced by Redlight Theatre, Toronto, 1977.

4 *Mother Country* (Toronto: Playwrights Canada, 1980), first produced at Tarragon Theatre Toronto, 1980.

5 *Operators/Bushed* (Toronto: Playwrights Canada, 1981). *Operators*, which has been revised, was first produced at New Play Centre, Vancouver, 1976; *Bushed* was first produced at Vancouver Playhouse, 1973.

THE APPLE IN THE EYE

Notes

The Apple in the Eye was originally written for radio and
broadcast by the CBC and the BBC in Australia and New
Zealand, and it has been translated and broadcast in several
European countries.

The first production of the stage version was at the 'Women
and Words' conference in Vancouver in 1983, directed by
Bonnie Worthington, with the following cast:
GEMMA *Judith Johns*
MARTIN *James McLarty*

Characters:
GEMMA *mid to late 20s.*
MARTIN *her husband, a little older.*

The staging of this play could be accomplished in many
different ways, but it would be more effective if Martin does
not appear on stage, and if the stage is bare of props and
furniture. Gemma should be wearing a pair of apple-green
pyjamas. Some method must be found to distinguish the
internal monologues from the actual conversation between
Gemma and Martin. It is suggested in the text that these are
marked by lighting changes, or perhaps the stream-of-
consciousness passages take place in a bright pool of light. An
enterprising director might find some other solution.

The Apple in the Eye

GEMMA *is alone on stage throughout. She is in bed, the light on her is dim. It is Sunday afternoon.*

GEMMA Martin?

MARTIN [*Voice only, offstage. Grunts.*]

GEMMA Martin!

MARTIN Gemma ... I'm reading, can't you see? I'm reading and listening to the game. I can't do three things at once. I can't listen to you and ... I can't keep my mind on ... Ssssh!

GEMMA [*Whispers.*] Mind? [*Lights up.*] If I were to take a very sharp knife and gently, so gently cut through my mind, how would it be? Soft and spongey like sodium? If I were to put it in water would it ride over the surface? Race around and burn itself out? No, I wouldn't let that happen. Keep the mind dry. My mind would be like an apple. [*Lights dim.*] Martin, give me a six letter word ending in *e* meaning secret.

MARTIN [*Automatically.*] Arcane.

GEMMA Never heard of it.

MARTIN Does it fit?

GEMMA Yes.

MARTIN Then it's right.

GEMMA [*Persisting*] Are you sure it's a word?

MARTIN Sssssh!

GEMMA How do you spell it – with a *c* or with a *k*?

MARTIN Sssssh!
[*Lights up.*]

GEMMA My husband Martin taught me to do crosswords. It's really very easy. I read out the clues. He gives me the answers. I do them in bed on a Sunday afternoon. [*Spells A-R-C-A-N-E.*] If I were to cut through the apple of my mind with a very sharp knife it would fall apart in two neat halves. [*Makes a cracking sound, perhaps with her thumb and finger.*]
[*Lights dim.*]

MARTIN What are you doing?

19

GEMMA Thinking.

MARTIN No you're not, you're cracking your fingers joints again, you know I can't stand that noise.
[*Lights up.*]

GEMMA ... in two neat halves. And there they would lie on the bed. On the green and orange sheets, which I shall burn next week because I am tired of orange and green dreams. The colours of a flag ... which one? I should ask my husband Martin. He is a collector of trivia. He hoards it and displays it at parties. The colour of a pineapple. My husband Martin can hold forth for ten minutes to any number of party goers.... [GEMMA *remembers* MARTIN *holding forth to a number of people. This may be* MARTIN*'s voice, recorded or distorted, or it may be spoken by* GEMMA *herself.*]

MARTIN Have you ever noticed the relationship between the eyes of a pineapple, which trace a logarithmic spiral, and the golden rectangle, which was familiar to the Ancient Greeks?

GEMMA ... and then he will go on to wonder whether this can also be applied to the strawberry ...

MARTIN [MARTIN*'s voice.*] An equally regular fruit.

GEMMA It's one of his party tricks. Some people produce white rabbits. Martin produces logarithmic spirals. And similar trivia.

MARTIN [MARTIN*'s voice, more intimate since he is not addressing so many people.*] Trivia? My dear Gemma, someone or something has master-minded the pineapple ... it is yet another indication of a defined order in the universe ...

GEMMA My husband Martin has a sneaking suspicion that God may be greater than computer science, since computer science has yet to come up with the perfect pineapple. A pineapple to me is simply orange and green. The colours of the girl's private school I was expelled from, for painting a phallus on the statue of the founder. The colours of some football team ...

COMMENTARY [*This may be recorded, or may be acted out by* GEMMA.] The Blue Bombers are on the Stampeders' 20-yard line. It's 2nd and 5, they come out of the huddle over the ball ...

GEMMA Are you really listening to that my love, my only love? Or is it simply background noise? The beating of a moth's wings on an outside pane. The beating of a mother's heart over the growing foetus. Have you ever considered that we are developed under the shadow of noise pollution? Boom. Boom. My husband Martin is extremely concerned over environmental noise. He is the chairman of our local branch of SPC. [*She spits this out, pronouncing it spuck (the Society for Pollution Control).*] He believes that the environment is doomed. There will be no more apples. [*Lights dim as she speaks to* MARTIN.] Give me an eight-letter word meaning giant mythological beast, ending in moth.

MARTIN Ssshhhhh.

GEMMA Giant, mythological ...

MARTIN [*Snaps.*] Behemoth.

GEMMA Behemoth. Large and portentous. Yes –

MARTIN What?

GEMMA Nothing. [*Lights up.*] Nothing, my love. You must understand that these are my own, my very private worries. Although they are trivial they are not interesting enough to add to your collection. What are such small worries when all around us the world is sinking, children with bloated bodies litter the TV screen ... and my mind lies in two neat halves on the green and orange sheet. [*Pause.*] One half of my mind contemplates the possibility of arcane amusements [*she giggles*], while the other half comes slowly to life, and the golden spider with eight-inch legs and a tiny diamond head nestling inside the etching, emerges and bites into the apple which is the two halves of my mind.

MARTIN You should take an aspirin, Gemma. Quit the crossword for a while.

GEMMA That was my husband. He's a very concerned man. The feeling of his hand on my forehead was received in perfect perspective by the now fractionally smaller but still exquisitely arcane half of my mind which lies on the centre of a large orange moon. Here beside me lies my husband Martin. Large and pale, since he works with

21

his mind and not with his body. [*Spells M-a-r ... a-t. Pause.*] Here beside me lies Marat in his bath. He has been bitten by the golden spider. His head drips blood, while into one ear, through a small plastic plug, flow the latest and greatest exploits of the Winnipeg Blue Bombers and the Calgary Stampeders. My only love.

COMMENTARY   [*May be recorded, or spoken by* GEMMA.] Stevens takes a snap – hands off to the fullback who hits the hole.

GEMMA   His lips twitch – have they scored? Or has the space-ship in the science-fiction novel which he is reading – taking care to hold it above the reddening water – has it taken off, hurling the intrepid earth-men towards greater and yet greater exploits in outer space? He is on page 53 of 'The last of the Tertians.' [*Pause.*] A large and nubile lady climbs out of the half of the apple which lies by my pillow. Saskia, wife of that artist in the velvet cap, with the kind squinty eyes. For a moment she stands poised on the edge of the bath. Poised ready to plunge. No, she's dragging Marat out of his bath, and the bluish light glances off the heavy folds of her bum. He's holding on. He doesn't want to leave. He's waving 'The last of the Tertians' above his head to keep it dry. She drags the ear piece from his ear, unhitches him ...
[*Lights dim.*]

MARTIN   Oh for God's sake Gemma. Can't you see I'm reading? Listening? Save it eh? Save it for 4.30. Take some medicine or something if you don't feel so good eh?
[*Lights up.*]

GEMMA   It is Sunday afternoon. On Sunday afternoon my husband Martin remains in bed, and, apart from infrequent visits to the bathroom, he has been up only once. He has put an overcoat over his pyjama legs, taken the Volkswagen from the underground car-park, and driven 23 blocks south, to the only shop in town where you can buy bagels and lox on a Sunday morning. Every Sunday morning he complains that in this town there are no Jewish ghettos, and if there were, there would be more shops stocking his Sunday morning manna. When he gets back it is my turn to rise, and he returns to bed. I undo the package, spread the bagels with cream cheese, arrange the lox on a plate with a small silver fork, and return to bed, carrying with me a perfect still life. My love destroys it with a single move. The cheese is squeezed between the warm yeasty folds. The lox is dangled aloft in a long pink tongue, and swallowed, seal fashion. Every week he complains that the bagels are not as good as the ones his mother made. [*Pause.*] Anyone who didn't know us might find this a carnal scene. It is not. My husband Martin is a computer scientist. He is an A.I. man. He is A.I. (To those who don't know, this stands for artificial intelligence, although those who do know might be right in thinking that artificial insemination is equally appropriate, particularly for my husband Martin.) He lectures. I'm told he is a very thorough lecturer.

RECORDING   [GEMMA *remembers* MARTIN *lecturing: (this may be* MARTIN'*s voice recorded, or it may be a recording of* GEMMA *impersonating* MARTIN*).*] Now I want you all to understand that this system is intended to be a general purpose generator for domains in a formalism similar to *FLIP*. The method used is close to *FLIP* but the search space is complete, unlike *FLIP* and several similar systems. The entire *LAYAWAY* programme, (that's *L-A-Y-A-W-A-Y*) comprises 52 clauses and aims at conciseness and clarity rather than efficiency. Nevertheless the present implementation solves some standard problems roughly 10 times faster than *FLIP*. *LAYAWAY* is perhaps interesting as a system implemented by first order logic, which solves problems in first order logic. [*Voice fades.*]

GEMMA   My husband Martin is a computer scientist greatly admired by his associates I am told. My husband Martin is.

RECORDING   [MARTIN'*s voice, or* GEMMA *impersonating him.*] Now you see my dear Gemma, I want you to understand that the gulf which divides us is simply due to a differing approach to the same problem. It may be solved quite simply by a slight adaptation on your part; it is a question of applying first order logic and a degree of systematization to your primary thought processes, which will then reflect on ...

MARTIN   [*Howls in anguish.*]

GEMMA [*Over last part of recording.*] Flip ... flip ... flip ... flip ...
[*Lights dim.*]

MARTIN Hey, just watch what you're doing with that ballpoint
pen Gem, you've messed up the crossword – just
missed my eye! What's the matter with you today?
[*Lights up.*]

GEMMA Saskia pulls Marat from his bath; it is like taking an
oyster from its shell. He lies and reads, oyster coloured,
flaccid ...

MARTIN [*Reads.*] The Tertian homed his laser on the target
reducing it to something that resembled finely
powdered human bone.

GEMMA Saskia leans over him. Seen in this light the two halves
of her buttocks are burnished, resembling nothing so
much as a golden delicious, split in half, each half lying
side by side, perfectly rounded, barely touching. A dark
stalk is hanging between the two halves. I pull the stalk,
the halves of my mind slam together with such an
impact that Marat pops into a new position. Propped up
at the banquet table he slurps his soup, and almost
swallows his spoon.
[*Lights dim.*]

MARTIN [*Coughing and choking.*] Oh Christ, hit me on the back
will you? [*Splutters.*] It's gone down the wrong way.
[*Coughs.*]
[*Lights up.*]

GEMMA On Saturday night before we go to bed I pop a pan of
corn and place it on the locker on Martin's side of the
bed in a cut glass bowl, ready for Sunday afternoon –
munchies, as Martin puts it.
[*Lights dim.*]

MARTIN [*Coughs.*]

GEMMA Better now love?

MARTIN [*Still spluttering, mumbles.*] Mmmmmmmmm.
[*Lights up.*]

GEMMA Saskia is under the table, under the snowy white folds of
the snowy white table cloth. Marat's pants reside
peaceably around his ankles. To all outward
appearances he is an invalid – wounded in some dark
arcane place, by a dark barb from which he has never
recovered. Propped up on

a satin pillow – barely able to eat, he splutters while
Saskia ... Saskia sucks. Not a muscle twitches. Not a sign
on his inert torso would indicate the pure arcane
delight which is occurring under the white cloth, under
the snowy whole folds. The behemoth swells as Saskia
sucks and Marat savours his soup. [*Lights dim.*]

MARTIN How come the popcorn ran out so quick this week
Gem? It's nearly finished.

GEMMA We're almost out of corn. I couldn've gone to the corner
store ...

MARTIN Sssh ... touchdown!
[*Lights up.*]

GEMMA Touchdown and blast off. The space ship passes into
orbit and Marat comes.

MARTIN Score! They scored!

GEMMA Saskia bucks. For a second the table is balanced on her
broad flanks – then it dumps back to earth and dishes
fly through the air in slow motion ... Marat sits. His legs
are all pappy, and he sits among the dishes, quite
unaware that the assembled company is staring at his
fallen pants, quite unaware of the huge, lard-like
woman, kneeling at his feet. He has more than soup in
his lap.
[*Lights dim.*]

MARTIN How about some tea honey?

GEMMA Did they make it?

MARTIN Who honey?

GEMMA Your team. Your team of course.

MARTIN Sure. Sure they made it. Too easy. Lousy game.

GEMMA You make it.

MARTIN Make what honey?

GEMMA The tea. You make the tea.

MARTIN I made it last week.

GEMMA So you did.

MARTIN Feeling better now sweet?

GEMMA Better?

MARTIN I thought you had a headache.

GEMMA That was last week.

MARTIN So it was.

25

[*Lights up.*]

GEMMA   I get out of bed and slide my feet into the sheepskin slippers my husband Martin bought for me for Christmas last year. I find it hard to walk. I look down. I am wearing the sheepskin slippers I bought for my husband Martin last Christmas. Last year he advised us to exchange utilitarian gifts. He is always afraid that I will spend more on him than he spends on me. His slippers are larger than mine, they contain more sheep, two dollars more, therefore in addition to my slippers, I received a pair of red wool and nylon socks. Martin buys his own socks. He wears pure wool. But to have bought me pure woolen socks would have meant spending more than two dollars. This was computed against the possibility of upsetting me with inferior quality, and the ticker tape decided that the possibility was minimal since I do not wear socks anyway. I take my right foot out of his left slipper, and there on my big toe is speared – a perfect apple.

I hobble into the kitchen, taking care to walk on my heels, and plug in the kettle. The apple waves to me. I turn down my toe and stub it violently against the linoleum. The apple splits into two perfect halves. One half stays still, staring at me benignly from two small pip-like eyes, the other skeeters across the floor under the kitchen table, where it is dark, dark and warm. I crawl underneath, but I can't find it. I hunch up and stay still, listening to the growl of the kettle as it prepares to boil. The noise is not unlike that of my mother's heart, which I cannot remember, but can feel, under the darkness of the table. The remaining half of the apple stares at me. Martin comes into the kitchen. My husband Martin has a doctorate in artificial intelligence. [*Lights dim, or* GEMMA *steps out of light.*]

MARTIN   Gemma, can't you hear that bloody kettle whistling?

GEMMA   [*Lights up, or* GEMMA *steps into light.*] Now one would imagine that with a degree in intelligence, even if it is artificial, one would be able to distinguish between a whistling kettle and an electric kettle, but apparently my only love cannot.

MARTIN [*Lights dim.*] There's steam all over the apartment.

GEMMA [*Lights up.*] Far away a train steams through an apple
orchard; it is spring, the flowers have not yet fallen – it is
somewhere in the south. Hot. I can hear the cicadas.
(Many years ago my husband Martin's upper teeth lost
out to somebody's foot in a football game. He now wears
dentures which he has a habit of clicking when he is
mad.) The flowers are painted with tiny delicate specks
of colour. Each speck lends itself to the whole, so that
the whole is not too much and not too little, all there,
absolutely right, each speck.

MARTIN [*Lights dim.*] Jesus Gemma, can't you do something
about that damned kettle?

GEMMA [*Lights up.*] My husband Martin is now shrouded in
steam.

MARTIN [*Lights dim.*] What are you doing Gemma? What are you
doing under the goddamned table? I thought you were
going to make the goddamned tea.

GEMMA Yes. Yes, I was. Only then you started swearing ...

MARTIN When? I wasn't swearing.

GEMMA Yes you were – you said goddamned.

MARTIN That was just now. I said it just now after you said you'd
make the tea.

GEMMA Mind your foot – don't step on my apple.

MARTIN What apple? Look, are you coming out from under that
goddamned table ...?

GEMMA There, you said it again.

MARTIN Or am I going to have to drag you out?

GEMMA [*Lights up.*] (My loved one likes to believe he's a cave
man.)

MARTIN [*Lights dim.*] All this is as a result of my trying to be fair.
You're pulling your little funnies again aren't you?

GEMMA [*Lights up.*] He stands. He stands, my beautiful
behemoth, guarding his cave. He shrugs; a man and a
woman look over one of his shoulders. What are they
looking at? Out over a vast expanse of water, with no
apparent interest. It is Sunday afternoon. There are
people in pairs picnicking by the side of the water. The
man and the woman stare, stiff and erect, he in a frock
coat and top hat, she in a dress with a bustle and an

absurd little black hat. A monkey plays at her feet ... and a dog. If you look closely you can see the tiny points of colour from which they are made – none of them touching. She holds a parasol. Para-for, sol-sun. Really two words. The parasol is growing, imperceptibly at first. I am the only one who notices as it grows, enveloping everything where everything is in pairs. Dog-monkey; boy-girl; lover-lover; man-woman; apple-apple; it is absolutely necessary for everything to be in pairs and for nothing to touch. Everything is stiff and formal, and nothing grows except the parasol which continues to spread and the woman with the starched face wants, oh she wants to make them all move, set them in motion. She runs her hand down the man's left thigh, slowly, nobody is looking. She moves it slightly to the right, he is not aware of her touch, his face remains stern, and then ... [*Lights dim.*]

MARTIN Ow! What are you doing? What are you doing with my pyjamas? Gemma!

GEMMA Joke!

MARTIN That's not funny. Come on out of there. And why don't you feed the cat once in a while? Look at her, she's half starved.

GEMMA She just ate.

MARTIN What did she eat?

GEMMA Lox. She ate your lox.

MARTIN She did not. I ate my lox.

GEMMA Then she must have eaten mine.

MARTIN I ate yours as well, don't you remember? You said you didn't want it.

GEMMA That was last week.

MARTIN Come off it Gemma, joke over.

GEMMA Stop shouting.

MARTIN I'm not shouting.

GEMMA If you go on shouting the neighbours'll find out we have a cat and we're not allowed to keep cats in this apartment.

MARTIN You don't deserve a cat. Letting it starve!

GEMMA You've got nothing on your feet. The floor's cold, you should put your slippers on.

MARTIN How can I? You're wearing them.

GEMMA Why don't you go back to bed Hon?

MARTIN I'm not moving till you come out of there.

GEMMA Be reasonable.

MARTIN Reasonable? When you spend half of Sunday under the kitchen table!

GEMMA Mind out!

MARTIN Mind what?

GEMMA You almost trod on it.

MARTIN What?

GEMMA The apple.

MARTIN What apple? What are you talking about Gemma? [*We might hear a scrape as he moves the table.*] Good God! Don't you ever clean under that table?

GEMMA You just performed a perfect lobotomy.

MARTIN It's filthy. Don't you ever get behind the furniture?

GEMMA What for?

MARTIN You're getting slovenly. You should watch yourself Gemma. [*We hear him pouring water.*] There you are – I've made the tea. You get the mugs and bring the tray back to bed.

GEMMA Sure. Yes. Okay. I'll do that.

MARTIN [*Distant.*] Good. Good. [*He closes the door.*] [*Lights up.*]

GEMMA Whew! That was a near thing. Now where did the other half go? I'm going to find you, other half. You can't go on hiding for ever. Ah, there you are, behind the stove. Hiding in the cobwebs. Got you. And we put the two together – so. Very gently ... Almost a perfect seal ... You're getting smaller. Now the tray he said ... And the mugs. We'll have the Mickey Mouse mugs just for a laugh. No ... He mightn't think it's funny. [*Lights dim as she calls.*] Martin? Should we have the Mickey Mouse mugs just for a laugh? Martin?

MARTIN Bring it in a goddamned samovar. I don't care.

GEMMA [*Carrying the tray.*] I'm sorry ... your game. You're listening to your game. Shall I move the popcorn? I said do you want the popcorn to stay on your stomach?

MARTIN [*Grunts.*]

GEMMA Okay, so I'll leave the popcorn. [*Lights up.*] Leave the

popcorn. Leave the popcorn and put the mug into one of the hands. The big, bony hands, veins protruding, hands in prayer. Marat in his bath never had such hands, strong, square hands, with square nails, well-etched lines, arced in prayer. No dirt under the praying nails. One hand holds the book open, the other holds the mug, one ear listens to the football game, the other listens to [*pause*] the A.I. The air is charged with A.I.A.I.-A.I.A.I. [*She intones as if in prayer.*] The Lord be praised for A.I., A-A-A-A- Men.
[*Lights dim.*]

MARTIN Pass the sugar will you?

GEMMA It's in the kitchen. I didn't bring the sugar.

MARTIN Well it's not sweet enough.

GEMMA I didn't sweeten it.

MARTIN Why not?

GEMMA I thought you did.

MARTIN How could you think that? You hadn't even taken the mugs off the shelf when ... oh damn!

GEMMA What?

MARTIN They scored.

GEMMA That's good ... isn't it?

MARTIN I don't know.

GEMMA You're not being logical Martin. Of course it's good.

MARTIN I didn't hear who did the scoring. I didn't hear who it was.

GEMMA Does it matter? As long as they scored. It's not as if you knew them personally.

MARTIN Ssssh.
[*Pause.*]

GEMMA I love Sundays.

MARTIN I used to.

GEMMA They haven't changed. Before we were married you spent Sundays in bed. You had bagels and lox and football and popcorn, and now you have me as well. Nothing's changed.

MARTIN Ssssshhh.

GEMMA [*Lights up.*] Nothing changes until 4:30, when the match ends and you turn onto your left hip and say 'how about it Gemma?' And I unbutton my pyjama jacket, and you take my left breast in your right hand and squeeze it till the nipple shows its face, and squeeze and squeeze until ... [*Makes a popping sound by putting her finger in her cheek*] out pops ... an apple. A tiny little apple ... and it bounces, yes, it bounces over the bedspread and onto the carpet and across the carpet and up into the window seat, and it sits and stares and you say –

MARTIN   [*As* GEMMA *steps out of light.*] What are you staring at Gemma?

GEMMA   [*In the light.*] And I say [*Out of light.*] ... only the apple in the window seat [*In light.*] and you say –

MARTIN   [*As* GEMMA *steps out of light.*] You've got goddamned apples on the brain today.

GEMMA   [*In light.*] And I say [*Out of light.*] You're right, oh how right you are ... you don't know how right you are. [*In light.*] And you say – [*In light.*] And I say – [*Out of light.*] Apple jelly. [*Pause, she takes her time getting back into the light.*] And I watch and wait for the apple over by the window to split open, and it waits for me to stop watching. It sits on the window seat, a determined little apple, wizened as hell, and it waits. And finally I throw back the sheet on my side of the bed. And you're pouring out a glass of sherry from the decanter we keep in your locker, since there isn't any sugar for your tea. And you put your sugarless tea in its Mickey Mouse mug on the floor beside the bed. The sherry is the same sherry we usually keep until after 4:30 when we both do what we do together, drink a glass of sherry, each, and I get up and I take a shower, and you get up and you take a shower, and I go into the living room and watch TV till it's time to get supper, and you go into the den and read A.I. or think A.I. or call up a colleague about A.I. and I watch TV and you ...

But you're drinking the sherry and it isn't 4:30, and you've switched off the game, and you watch me over the brim of your glass as I get out of bed and walk over to the window, and pick up the apple and walk over to your side of the bed, and brush your mug with my foot, and I'm not looking at your invitation, I'm walking towards you, with the apple sitting on the palm of my hand, and I reach you, and I drop it into your glass, and you take one last gulp, and swallow it down. Whole. BLACKOUT.

EVER LOVING

Notes

Ever Loving has been performed in Halifax, Montreal, Toronto and Vancouver. This play was first produced at the Belfry Theatre, Victoria, BC with the following cast:

RUTH WATSON (RUTHIE) *Alison MacLeod*
JAMES MICHAEL O'SULLIVAN (DAVE) *William Dunlop*
PAUL TOMACHUCK *Robert Seale*
DIANA MANNING *Donna Carroll White*
CHUCK MALECARNE *Blaine Parker*
LUCE MARIA MARINI *Angela Fusco*
Director: James Roy

Author's Note: The action of the play takes place between 1938 and 1970. The set should be flexible, at one time or another it represents a bar, a café, three railways stations, a train, a farm, various domestic interiors, La Gondola (an Italian supper club), etc. Costume changes are quick indicators of changes of period and leaps in time and it is recommended that costumes be as realistic as possible.

Act I, Scene One

In 'La Gondola,' a supper club in Niagara Falls, 1970.
Italian decor. DIANA, PAUL, RUTH, *and* DAVE *are eating in*
silence at a table illuminated by a single candle. DIANA's
accent is less pronounced than in the following scenes,
and PAUL *has picked up a slightly British intonation.* LUCE
sits nearby smartly dressed and coifed, alone at a table.
CHUCK *is playing and singing, his style exaggeratedly*
Mediterranean, smooth. He sings 'I Never Promised You
a Rose Garden' in Italian.

DIANA   Well, this is really nice. [*Smiles. Silence.* DIANA *pats*
    PAUL's *hand.*]

RUTH   I still have your fur. It's a bit yellow, but it's all right. I've
    kept it in tissue. Do you want it back?

DIANA   I'd forgotten about it.

DAVE   [*Prodding his meat.*] What is this anyway?

RUTH   It's veal. You've had it before.

DAVE   Yeah ... I mean the sticky stuff.

DIANA   Marsala – it's a sauce.

DAVE   Mmmm.

DIANA   This is all such a revelation to me. [DIANA *smiles. She is*
    far more socially at east then RUTH *and* DAVE.]

PAUL   D'you know Dave, this is the first trip we've ever taken
    out east ...

DIANA   [*To* RUTH.] Apart from that dreadful train ride – you
    remember? [*Pauses.*] Niagara Falls. We planned it as a
    silver wedding gift to each other. [*Pauses.*] In another
    five years we'll be retiring to the west coast – [*To* PAUL.]
    somewhere around '75, isn't that right? Paul's been
    having a bit of trouble with the old war wound, so
    there's no sense pressing our luck.

PAUL   Yes. Going to try some city living for a change – Victoria.
    [*To* RUTH.] Ever been there?

RUTH   No.

DAVE   [*Suddenly, to* PAUL.] Seems to me you were a bit of a

womanizer, isn't that right? I was looking for you in the
old regimental photograph – you weren't there.

PAUL We weren't in the same regiment.

RUTH I told you that.

DIANA Well it's so nice to know that we've all done so well.

PAUL [*Pouring wine.*] Come on – try some of this. My wife
claims it's a good vintage, don't you Di? [*Holds the
bottle up to* LUCE, *mistaking her for the hostess.*] Waiter
... another bottle. [*To* DAVE.] It's all right, it's on us. We're
celebrating.

DAVE [*Preventing* PAUL *from pouring into* RUTH's *glass.*] It
doesn't agree with her.

CHUCK [*TO* LUCE.] Friends of yours?

LUCE I never set eyes on them.

CHUCK Just as well. I wouldn't wanna know you if they were.

LUCE Snob!

CHUCK Just choosy, that's all. Always was. [*Touches* LUCE's
hand.*]

DIANA It was an inspiration thinking of you, wasn't it, Paul?

PAUL Sure was.

DIANA And then finding you at the same address. As soon as
we got here I called directory assistance for Hamilton. I
couldn't think of your married name. All I could think of
was Watson. Ruthie Watson.

RUTH O'Sullivan. [*Prods her food.*] It's Irish.

DIANA Yes. [*Nods at* RUTH's *food.*] Aren't you enjoying it?

RUTH We don't come out to restaurants very often.

PAUL Neither do we. [*To* DIANA.] When did we last eat out?

DIANA We only have one good restaurant within a hundred
miles. My brother came over a few years ago ... I think
that's what bugged him most. It's funny what you can
get used to. Paul went through hell with me the first
year or two, didn't you?

PAUL Well ... I guess all the girls put up a bit of a fight didn't
they? [*Pauses.*] So ... did you make it to Expo?

DAVE No ... no, we didn't bother.

PAUL We're planning to look in – better late than never, eh?

DAVE They coulda spent that money on something better.
Stamp out crime across the country, eh, Ruthie?

RUTH Aye.

PAUL You a cop?

DIANA I was a policewoman during the war.

DAVE You?

RUTH He's a security guard.

PAUL Good job?

DAVE Security officer. Lousy pay but I'm not complaining. You don't see us going on strike. We do that and the whole goddamn country falls apart. [*Blows out the candle on the table.*] Biggest fire hazard there is. Yeah ... [*To* DIANA.] Look where strikes got your country ... down the drain. [RUTH *is searching in her purse.*] [*TO* RUTH.] What are you looking for?

RUTH Matches. [*To* DIANA.] I didn't bring any. [DAVE *gives* RUTH *a thunderous look.*]

DIANA I'll do it. [*Lights the candle.*]
[*Pause.*]

DIANA Well ... it's been a long time eh? A heck of a time. Too long of course ... Yes ... well, nothing comes easily does it? I can't say I'd've changed anything though – looking back. It's extraordinary really. I don't know where the years've gone.
[*They all stare into the flame. The lights dim.*
Searchlights sweep across the stage accompanied by an air raid siren and blackout. The three couples dive offstage. The scene is struck in a frenzy of activity. The siren dies and an ominous silence prevails. 'All clear' is heard. The sound of the sea as the lights come up a little. Music – 'Will Ye Ne'er Come Back Again.' The voice of COLONEL W.E. SUTHERLAND. O.B.E., *Commander of the* Queen Mary, *is heard. He has an English accent.*]

COLONEL Ladies and gentlemen, this is your captain speaking. In less than an hour we will be docking in Halifax. Canada is just ahead and I want particularly to address this message to all of you who are representative of the true flower of English womanhood. Canada's fighting men have placed their trust in you, and I am confident that you and your lovely children, the like of whom I have rarely seen, will not betray this trust. The dark years are over. Your courage, sacrifice and bravery have helped to make victory possible. You have won the admiration of

decent peoples throughout the world ... [COLONEL
SUTHERLAND'S *voice begins to fade.*] Canada welcomes
you as citizens of whom she may be justly proud ...
[*Lights up on* CHUCK, *at home, practising 'Don't Sit
Under the Apple Tree.' Lights fade.*]

Scene Two

*Fall, 1945. Onstage we see a Union Jack and three railway
stations: Halifax, Hamilton, and Regina. In Halifax, a
banner reads 'Welcome to Canada British War Brides.'
LUCE sits brooding under the banner. There is also a
wartime poster which should show the Canadian,
American and British heads of state. DIANA and RUTH
enter. They have luggage. RUTH has a baby in a carry-cot.
They walk past LUCE, looking for the train.*

DIANA It's over there – that must be it.
RUTH Are you sure? If we get on the wrong one we might end
up with the Eskimos. [*Pauses.*] Shall I ask? [*Glances at
LUCE.*]
DIANA I doubt if she'd know. Don't stare.
RUTH Why wouldn't she know?
DIANA She doesn't look English.
RUTH Well, none of them are.
[*They stop and examine the poster.*]
RUTH Look, there's Mr. Churchill and President thingamabob
in his wheelchair – who's that one?
DIANA That's their prime minister I think. King –
RUTH King what?
DIANA Ruthie!
RUTH He doesn't look like a prime minister. [*Glances back at
LUCE.*] It's awful ... *foreign* isn't it, I mean ...
[*They get in the train and settle themselves. The lights
dim. The train is in motion. LUCE is still wrapped in her
cape, at the station. CHUCK, at home, plays a snatch of
'Sentimental Journey'.*]
DIANA [*Indicating a paper bag which RUTH is holding.*] What's
that?

RUTH Oh ... nothing.

DIANA It's dripping.

RUTH Yes. [*Sniffs it.*] It's maybe a bit mouldy. Well, I couldn't eat it on the boat. I couldn't let it go to waste ... all that real white bread, and cornflakes ... and did you see the tinned peaches? It's not fair I had to go and get seasick.

DIANA But you can't keep the stuff. The train meals are enough for an army.

RUTH Aye ... I suppose.

DIANA Here ... let me throw it out of the window.

RUTH No ... no ... maybe someone'll want it.
[*Pause.* DIANA *stares out the window.*]

RUTH What's he going to think of me – I haven't slept for three nights. I look like a witch.

DIANA You look all right to me.

RUTH Aye, but you don't know me. You don't know how nice I can look.

DIANA We've been in pretty close proximity for the last three weeks.
[*Pause.*]

RUTH I shouldn't've put my frock on in Halifax. [*Looks out the window.*] It's not very green is it ... Not *green* green – more black.

DIANA Fir trees.

RUTH Aye. And do you know they're full of bears. Dave told me. I wonder what the cows eat? It's all trees.

DIANA Lovely colours. They must be maples ... See ... those red ones. That's their national tree.

RUTH National *tree*? [*Thinks.*] We've got the thistle.

DIANA They call autumn fall.

RUTH It feels ... different. Creepy. Foreign. [*Pauses, has no word to express her feelings.*] Big.

DIANA Don't look at it.

RUTH I can't help it.

DIANA [*Irritated.*] Well don't.

RUTH Don't shout at me.
[*Pause.* RUTH *is near to tears.*]

DIANA [*Sighs.*] It's going to take time isn't it? Getting the hang of ... [*Makes an expansive gesture.*]

RUTH Oh, it'll be all right – as soon as I see Dave – as soon as I

see my house. He's going to love Rita. [*Pauses.*] How
many are you going to have?

DIANA We've decided on two. I'd like a boy and a girl.

RUTH You can't stop them coming just like that.

DIANA Oh we're not catholics.

[RUTH *grimaces. They stare out the window. The sound of
a train whistle. In the distance, strains of 'The Wedding
March' are heard.*]

RUTH They're playing it again. Someone's getting out.

DIANA [*Getting up to look.*] It's not even a station! There's not a
house in sight. There's someone with a violin. How jolly.
[*Hums along.*]

RUTH We're not brides. Half the women are pregnant.

DIANA Pour soul. She's crying.

RUTH [*Not looking.*] Yes.

DIANA There's four or five fellows out there to meet her.
They're all kissing her on both cheeks. That's the way
the French do it. Whoops – we're off. [*Lurches back into
seat.*] I'm glad it wasn't me.
[*They sit in silence.*]

Scene Three

Halifax Station, fall, 1945.

CHUCK Come on, Loose. I don't get it. Why do you have to
spend all your time on the railway station?

LUCE People.

CHUCK Well, there's people at home. All you gotta do is walk to
the corner store to see people. Go downstairs and talk
to Mama once in a while. She's people. She'll be glad to
show you what's what.

LUCE People, la gente. Vengano, vanno. Dove vanno?

CHUCK What?

LUCE Where they go? La gente?

CHUCK How should I know? On journeys – they're travelling.

LUCE Stranieri. Da dove? Where from they come? Are my
brothers. Fratelli. Tutti fratelli.

CHUCK Where?

LUCE [*Vaguely.*] Là.

Scene Three

CHUCK I'm your brother! [LUCE *stares at him.*] Goddammit, Loose. I'm not coming down to the railway station every day to bring you home for supper.

LUCE Non è necessario. I come back. Sola. [*Makes no move.*]

CHUCK So what do you think Mama and Papa are thinking? They're thinking you're not happy with me. With us. Well, if you'd rather spend your days here ... [LUCE *shrugs.*] This is the last time I'm coming looking for you. Okay? You just come home.

LUCE Home?

CHUCK Casa. Casa mia. Okay? Now! [*Leaves.*]

Scene Four

Fall, 1945. RUTH *and* DIANA *are still on the train.*

DIANA It's all ... untouched. London's horrible now ... ugly. Here everything's so splendidly ... untouched. No bombing ... nothing destroyed ... mile upon mile ... well, there's nothing to bomb is there? There's no one to kill.

RUTH Bears.

DIANA It's quite beautiful really.

RUTH Yes. But it's not like Scotland.

DIANA Space. That's what Paul said. A blank page just waiting for us to write on. [*Shakes her head.*] I thought I understood him. Did you notice that Canadian in the restaurant car this morning? He was reading a comic. A grown man!

RUTH Yes ... Dave likes comics. I hope he'll be able to meet me. I hope his family likes me. What if they don't? What'll you do if Paul's don't like you?

DIANA Oh, they will. There might be a slight problem with the father not speaking fluently ... he's Ukrainian.

RUTH What's that?

DIANA Oh ... a part of Russia. Luckily I speak German. We won't be seeing much of Paul's family, anyway. They're country people. Farmers. Paul's not like that. [*Pauses.*] I hope he's not crippled. He says he's all right but ...

RUTH I'd'a died if Dave'd got hurt.

41

DIANA He writes these incredible letters. I shall miss them.

RUTH They'll think I look all right, won't they? [*Looks at her dress.*] My mother helped me alter it. She got it off a friend who died.

DIANA Was she a big woman? The friend?

RUTH Big? Aye, she was bonny, why?

DIANA Nothing.

RUTH It's the shoulders, isn't it?

DIANA I'll tell you what. I'll give you something to go with it. [*Gets her case from under the seat.*] There ... [*Brings out a white fox wrap.*]

RUTH [*Overwhelmed.*] Oh! ...

DIANA Go on. Try it on.

RUTH No. No, I couldn't.

DIANA I don't need it. It's hot on the prairies.

RUTH Aye. It's hot in Hamilton too – when it's not snowing. [*Tries on the wrap.* RUTH *fantasizes. Music – a Viennese waltz.* RUTH *wears a tiara and waltzes wearing the wrap, tosses a single rose to an admirer. Fantasy ends.*] If I could borrow it ... I could maybe post it back to you ...

DIANA It's yours.
[*Pause.* RUTH *gets the feel of the wrap. She takes it off with a quick gesture.*

RUTH I can't take it. [*Bursts into tears.*]

DIANA [*Hugs* RUTH.] Oh Ruthie.

RUTH You don't have to be so nice to me ... It's all so ... so ...

DIANA It's going to be all right. Don't worry. We've got to make it all right. They'll be waiting for us – as long as we love them nothing else matters.

RUTH I don't know. I don't know ...

Scene Five

PAUL *and* DAVE *are waiting for the train at Regina and Hamilton stations.* PAUL *has flowers. Their monologues should run over each other, though some phrases should stand alone.*

DAVE What's taking her so long? Shouldn't have to wait like this ... You watching over me Rita? [*Pats his pocket.*] You

better be ... Why the hell didn't I get a photograph? How
come she sent me a picture of the kid when I asked for
one of her? Does that mean she's fat? Jesus! What if I
don't recognize her? What if she's fat? What if she
doesn't love me ... loves the kid and ... Well if she doesn't
love me I won't love her ... eh Rita? That's only right isn't
it? Verna. Why does she keep hanging around? Should'a
told her about ... about the kid. What's she gonna say?
She'll make a big scene. Jesus! Well, I wasn't engaged to
her or nothing. She can't fool me she was waiting
around for me ... I don't care what she said in her letters
I know what she was doing ... Well Jackie Cranmer as
good as he said it didn't he? Even with my own brother
... no ... [*Pauses.*] Hope she doesn't want me to finish
high school. No, she won't want that. If only Dad coulda
held out another couple of months. Wish she'd get here.
Hold my hand Rita ... hold my hand ...

PAUL God she can't hate it ... she'll love it ... she'll go along
with ... we can build it up together ... So why doesn't she
wanna talk about it in her letters? God! She can't hate it.
What if she's changed? People don't change ... yes they
do ... No – that's crazy. Look on the bright side. Well,
we're still the same people – underneath – she's the
same person. I'm ... oh, God! For ever and ever ... I'll
never get to sleep on my own again. It's gonna be okay.
Isn't it? Hell, we'll get old together ... we'll read books in
the winter, yeah, that's it, read out loud, I'll read to her
when she gets near-sighted, she can nurse me when I'm
sick ... What if I do get sick? Yeah, we'll read
Shakespeare. Why doesn't she get here? [*Suddenly.*]
She's not coming. Well, I can get by without a woman –
sure, I mean, I never laid a hand on one of those nurses
did I? Never. How come? Don't remember. Maybe I'm
undersexed. Jees! It'll be okay when she gets here. She's
that kind of person, makes things happen. None of the
great philosophers were married were they? Didn't have
wives ... Kant, Heidegger, did Buddha get married? Wish
there'd never been a war ... wish I'd never been over
there. Wish I'd stayed.

Scene Six

Fall, 1945, on the train. DIANA *is looking at the baby.*

DIANA   I think she's hungry.

RUTH   Aye ... it's time ... I'll go and warm the bottle.

DIANA   Should we wake her?

RUTH   Of course. It's time.

DIANA   Let me do it.

RUTH   No ... thanks all the same.

DIANA   Just once more.

RUTH   Everyone's wondering whose baby she is –

DIANA   I know but ...

RUTH   So I'll do it.

DIANA   I have been rather hogging her –

RUTH   It's all right. You can practise on your own one. [*Tries to pass* DIANA.]

DIANA   Ruthie ... do you mind if I ask you something – it's a bit silly – I mean, I was always giving advice to people before ... but it was all so, sort of abstract. [*Suddenly.*] Did it hurt?

RUTH   What?

DIANA   Having her? She's got such a big head.

RUTH   She has not!

DIANA   You don't have to talk about it.

RUTH   Ach, we all talk about it when we get together up the train. Haven't you listened?
[DIANA *shakes her head.*]

RUTH   It wasn't as bad as some of them make out. I'd've liked it better if Dave'd been there with me though.

DIANA   Don't be silly – men are far too squeamish.

RUTH   Not Dave. He says that after what he's seen nothing'll set him back.

DIANA   [*Doubtful.*] I don't think I'd like Paul to be in on it.

RUTH   Yes you will.

DIANA   My father never came within two hundred miles of my mother when she had us.

44

Scene Six

RUTH Aye, but they're old-fashioned.

DIANA We were twins.

RUTH You and your brother? You never said –

DIANA We weren't that close.

RUTH Won't you miss him?

DIANA Hugh? No, of course not.

RUTH No?

DIANA To hell with all of them anyway. [*Bites her lip.*]

RUTH Here ... you can take her. [RUTH *pushes the baby into*
DIANA'*s arms.* DIANA *clings to the baby, rocking it
closely.*] Just this one last time, mind ...
[DIANA *leaves, carrying the baby.* RUTH *is left alone in the
carriage.*]

Scene Seven

As the scene begins, RUTH *and* DIANA *are on the train and*
LUCE *is still at Halifax station, 1945. After the first three
speeches, the scene changes to 1938.* RUTH *is in a fish
shop,* DIANA *on a tennis court, and* LUCE *at home.*

RUTH [*Staring out the window of the train.*] I wonder how
many of my friends've got babies? They'll all have gone
back to the fish market now that the war's over.
[*Defiantly.*] Well, I'm glad I'm not in their boat.

DIANA [*Elsewhere on the train, imitating the train, rocking the
baby.*] Da da da dum, da da da dum, da da da dum. One
da da equals about two feet, say, da dum equals two
more feet, how many feet in a mile, five thousand two
hundred and eighty? Multiplied by how many miles? ...

LUCE [*On the platform, mesmerised.*] Treni, guardando ... i
treni ... guardanado, treni passando – passare la vita
guardando treni – sognando, sognando, tanti sogni ...
sogni ... sogni – dreams. [*Hisses very softly, as if letting
out steam.*]
[*Scene changes to 1938. Music – 'Bonny Dundee.'*]

RUTH [*Scaling fish.*] It's not fair. Maggie's been on the counter
for over a month and you promised me you'd get me off
scaling. I'm going as fast as I can, Mr. MacKie – well, you

45

promised. [*To girl beside her.*] He'd have us here all
night if he could.
[*Music – 'Il Lombardino,' an Italian folk song.*]

LUCE [*With an English textbook.*] Il mio nome ... my name is
Luce Maria Marini ... How do you do? [*Closes the book
and closes her eyes, trying to memorize.*] I am Luce
Maria Marini. [*Extends her hand.*] How do you do ...
Yank? I am mighty fine. [*Closes the book.*]
[*Music – 'Hearts of Oak.'*]

DIANA [*On the tennis court, playing, shout.*] Love-fifteen. I'm
sure Anthony. Really. [*To herself.*] Why aren't you more
mysterious? What if you spoke with an accent? Come in
to ze Casbah. [*Giggles.*] Well at least you could learn to
roll your 'r's. Maybe they'll make you in the navy. The
war might be good for something! Come on!

LUCE I have twenty – one, two – twenty-two years. [*Calls out,
answering her mother's shout.*] Si, vengo Mama, vengo.

RUTH [*Looks at clock.*] Ten past two. Will Andy take me to the
pictures tomorrow night? There's Jeanette MacDonald
and Nelson Eddy on ... 'Your eyes are like two spoonfuls
of the blue Pacific.'

DIANA It might even liven things up a bit 'round here. Daddy
doesn't think so. He has too much business with
Germany. Well, they're not really *enemy*. How can they
be? They can capture me any day! Must try not to think
about it. It's such an awful word ... war. [*To Anthony.*]
Out!

LUCE Dicono che ci sarà una guerra. [*Looks up the word.*]
Warrr. Will to be warrra. They say ... no? Is true, Yank? E
vero? You want me to come to bed? [*Giggles at her
audacity, opens book.*]

RUTH Five more minutes and I'll shut one eye, then if I sit on
the stool for ten minutes ... He's given me these spots on
my chin. Clark Gable wouldn't rub my chin. He'd go
straight for my lips. I hope I wouldn't get lipstick on
him. [*Dreams.*]

LUCE I like New York.

DIANA Now Hugh's been called up ... I wouldn't mind being a
pilot, if he can do it why can't I?
[*The three women begin to speak in concert; an
occasional phrase can stand alone.*]

RUTH Oh, Humphrey! He comes straight for me and touches
my face. 'You're exquisite,' and everyone hears and he
doesn't care. 'You're coming away with me, doll.' 'Oh
Humphrey, how can I? ... What about Andy?' His eyes
burn and I think he's going to kiss me, but instead I feel
him slipping a ring on my finger and I almost faint. And
he carries me to his Rolls Royce and drives me to
Hollywood and we sit in his mansion and sip green
goddesses and talk about our love.

LUCE Here women is making only bambini, more bambini! Is
nothing other to make. In America ... [*Dreams herself
into perfect English.*] For Christ's sake tell those people
to stop following me ... and there is no one can tell me I
can't smoke. It is my voice. Mine. My apartment. My
manager. I'm just too busy. And I don't give autographs!

DIANA Last summer in Heidelberg ... the boys were fabulous ...
Are you sure you wouldn't like to take a breather
Anthony? Fabulous – just the way I always imagined.
Fantabulous dancers ... frightfully ... masculine ... in that
sort of ... German way. Not a bit like English men. Why
do you let your mouth hang open when you serve?
[*Concert speaking ends.*]

LUCE I want to go to America!

RUTH [*Looks at the clock.*] An hour and three quarters.
[*Changes feet.*]

DIANA Out!
[*Concert speaking resumes.*]

RUTH When I get married, I'll have a bedroom with a dressing
table with three mirrors and a frill on the bottom, and
I'll have four bridesmaids in pink dresses. [*Looks at the
clock.*] An hour and a half.

LUCE I will to be cantatrice. [*Sings.*] You like? I like you, Yank. I
like to go to New York. Non è possibile. E cattiva – orni
giorno ... take lesson make practise, hello Mama, hello
Papa, eat food, stay house, learn English, for what? Ogni
giorno lo stesso. Same. No thing to make. Che noioso. In
American non è così. My mother wishes I sposare ...
marry with Angelo ... my cugino – cowsin. Non voglio,
non voglio sposarmi. I will not marry with Italian boy. I
marry with American man. You come to bed, Yank?

DIANA   I always did like foreign men, I don't know why. That's game and set Anthony, I hated to do it to you. [*Smiles broadly. Concert speaking ends.*]

RUTH   [*Looks at clock.*] An hour and fifteen minutes!

LUCE   Dicono che ci sarà una guerra ... warrr!

DIANA   [*Laughs.*] War? Oh how silly. It can't possibly last!

Scene Eight

Scene shifts between CHUCK *in Halifax, 1941, and* DAVE *in Hamilton Station, 1939. Both are in new uniforms.* CHUCK *is at home, practising 'There'll Always Be an England' throughout the scene.*

CHUCK   [*Sings the first line in a blank, neutral voice.*] No ... no ... boring! This could be my big break. Well, there's never been a war where they didn't need music. [*Croons the first couple of lines of the song.*] Close, but no cigar! [CHUCK *fantasizes. He is in a spotlight. Caruso-like he soars above a huge choir or orchestra version of 'There'll Always Be an England.' Fantasy lights dim on* CHUCK, *lights up on* DAVE, *in uniform, on Hamilton Station, 1939.*]

DAVE   Jeeze – won't they ever run on time again? [*Looks at his watch. Paces. Pacing becomes marching. Comes to attention, salutes.*] I got shoes that fit and they're not my Dad's hand-me-downs. I got a uniform ... I got a job ... [*Throws his hat in the air.*]
[*Fantasy lights up on* CHUCK, *who bows to the sound of waves of applause. Fantasy lights down, normal lighting up.*]

CHUCK   Paris ... Rome ... Berlin, here I come!
[DAVE *fantasizes.*]

DAVE   How we gonna get there? Troop ship from Halifax. [*Salutes.*] For king and country. [*Dives onto his stomach and defends his position with a gun. Crawls on his stomach.*] For the British Empire! Okay, Johnny ... hold on there while I defuse this mine ...
[*The mine explodes.* DAVE *looks up and sees Mackenzie King.*]

Scene Eight

DAVE Mr. Prime Minister, sir! [*Assumes the voice of Mackenzie King.*] 'Welcome back to Canada, son. It's been a long year.' [DAVE's *voice.*] Thank you Mr. King, sir. [*Mackenzie King's voice.*] 'What can we do for you?' [DAVE's *voice.*] I just wanna carry on, sir – some kinda work like I been doing, to suit my talents. [*Mackenzie King's voice, in a confidential whisper.*] 'Well, it just so happens we need someone to test this new fighter plane and I think you're our man ...' [CHUCK *plays 'There'll Always Be an England.'*]

CHUCK Canadian guy wrote it, so a Canadian guy can sing it, right? [*Tries a new style, sings.*] 'The empire too, we can depend on you ...' [*Glances across at* DAVE, *ends with a crashing chord.*]

Scene Nine

A dingy English café, 1941. PAUL *and* DIANA *face each other, drinking tea.* PAUL, *nervous, sticks his finger out as he drinks.*]

DIANA Why are you doing that?

PAUL What?

[DIANA *sticks her finger out.* PAUL *spills his tea. He is tongue-tied, embarrassed.*]

DIANA Oh, it's all right. It'll wash. You don't have to drink it you know. I won't be offended. [PAUL *puts his cup aside gratefully.*] It's not a very good brand – dusty. Shall I be mother? [*Refills his cup.*] You should have seen this place two years ago. They had lovely china and lace cloths and real cream.

PAUL Really?

DIANA Yes. You really should've seen it before the war. [*Silence.*] Have you been to Europe before? [PAUL *shakes his head.*] What were you doing before you joined up?

PAUL I used to read a lot.

DIANA No ... I mean work? What did you work at? [PAUL *shrugs. Silence.*]

PAUL Look ... I ... I don't know why you invited me.

DIANA You said you were lonely.

PAUL Yes ... but ...

DIANA Well it's not such a big event. We're only having tea ...

PAUL I'm sorry.

DIANA That's all right.

PAUL Why did you join the police?

DIANA My mother thought it was safer – if she only knew!
[*Laughs.*] I was going to join the WAFs actually – that's
what I've always wanted to do – fly, or explore the
Amazon in a boat – well, I suppose everybody does.

PAUL The Amazon?

DIANA I mean who wants to stick around here all their life? If
the war hadn't happened I was enrolled in a secretarial
college. I was going to be a bilingual secretary – you
know, French and German. Maybe work in France ... Do
you?

PAUL What?

DIANA Know French and German?

PAUL Only Ukrainian.

DIANA What?

[PAUL *shrugs.*]

DIANA But why? I mean ... Ukrainian?

PAUL My old man came over from the Ukraine in twenty-
three. He brought my mother. They didn't speak
English. My dad doesn't speak too much of it even now.

DIANA Well why doesn't he learn?

PAUL Never had to I guess. He had to break land, no one to
talk to. Mom died when I was a little kid ... No medical
facilities or anything. We were out in the sticks, see –
still are come to that.

DIANA What sticks?

PAUL What?

DIANA Sticks?

PAUL Oh ... it means nowhere. You know?

DIANA Say something. Go on.

PAUL I have.

DIANA In Ukrainian.

PAUL No, I can't. I don't want to have anything to do with that.
[*Pauses, then suddenly.*] Tea dusza krasna. [*Shrugs,
confused.*]

DIANA Then you must be a farmer too.

PAUL Me? [*Suddenly animated.*] Not me. You wouldn't get me near a farm.

DIANA What then? Let me look at your hands. Come on ... I'll guess.
[PAUL *puts a hand on the table, then pulls it away suddenly.*]

PAUL I was gonna be a printer. I had an opportunity. It wasn't exactly what I wanted but it was a job ... We were printing a translation of Goethe. Poetry ... and then ...

DIANA Well you can always go back to it. Goethe'll always be there.

PAUL No he won't. I won't go back there.

DIANA Why is everyone so negative? Of course you'll go back.

PAUL They stopped the printing. He was a German. Anyway, I got fired.

DIANA Oh? Why?

PAUL For printing ... something I shouldn't'a been.

DIANA What?

PAUL Illegal material.

DIANA What kind? [*Pause.*] Paul? [*Pause.*] Paul?

PAUL [*Looking away.*] Pamphlets – stuff like that. They got this War Measures Act, see. So they can stomp on everyone – Close the meeting halls, shut down the presses – they have informers.

DIANA Who's they?

PAUL The government, who else? The goddamned Liberals – oh, I'm sorry.

DIANA That's all right. I'm not made of gossamer you know.

PAUL It's never gonna happen again – I'll tell you – if this war changes anything it'll change that ... bourgeois tyranny.

DIANA I don't understand.

PAUL Communism – what would you know about that? Communism – I had a job – when you were sixteen you wanted to fly. I had a job and when they found out I got turned in, some s.o.b. turned me in, kaput, finished, they sent me back to the farm, there was nowhere else to send me, was there? So there. There you are – I told you didn't I. I was a communist.

DIANA I think that's fantastic.

PAUL [*Taken aback.*] You do?

DIANA My father'd have a fit! He's terrified of commies ...

PAUL Sssssh!

DIANA Be like dad, keep mum. [*Puts her finger over her lips, imitating a wartime poster, then tries to stop giggling.*]

PAUL My old man, he used to be pretty active in the old country, left wing stuff of course, still talks a lot but he licks the Anglicki's boots, yes. Sold out for the land, sold himself, and licks their boots even though he hates their guts. You can't talk to him, he never listens, goes ahead and does what he thinks, talk, talk, talk, talk and he never even listens.

DIANA What's an Anglicki?

PAUL [*Not listening.*] But I'm not gonna do that. Shall I tell you something? I'm going to be a writer, I'm going to write it all down, tell about Estevan and the strikes, they shot them all on the street you know, I'm gonna write – I don't tell that to everyone. In fact, you're the first person I've told.

DIANA Paul? What's an Anglicki?

PAUL Aglicki? English of course.

DIANA [*Stiffly.*] You don't like the English?

PAUL I didn't say that did I? I got nothing against England as long as it stays right here – I volunteered didn't I? When this war's over there's a few things gonna change ... it's the end of imperialism, all that stuff's dead. Canadians aren't licking any more boots ... if I'm still alive I'll ...

DIANA [*Standing.*] Well, I've really enjoyed this. I have to go now.

PAUL [*Confused.*] You do?

DIANA I'm on duty at four ...

PAUL Yes but you said ...

DIANA [*Puts her gloves on.*] Bye-bye Paul. [*Holds out her hand briefly, then starts to leave.*]

PAUL Here ... here, I brought you something. I didn't like to give it to ... here ... [*Takes out a chocolate bar and thrusts it at her.*]

DIANA [*Unenthusiastic.*] Chocolate. How nice ...

PAUL I can get more ... They told me that all the English girls ...

DIANA Yes.

Scene Nine

[*Awkward pause.*]

PAUL What I said in Ukrainian ...

DIANA I must go. [*Leaves.*]

PAUL I said you were beautiful. [*Puts his head in his arms.*]
[*This scene melds into the next, as least as far as* PAUL's *line in Scene Ten.*]

Scene Ten

CHUCK *and* LUCE's *room, Halifax, 1946.* LUCE *stares out the window. She is deeply depressed.*

CHUCK Loose. Hey, Loose. [*Waves, tries to attract her attention.*]

PAUL Anglicki.

CHUCK Here. Here ... I got you something. Dictionary. Help you to know the words. Come on, Loose ... ah, c'mon. I know you don't have to be like this. It doesn't fool me. Come on, Loose. [*Embraces her.*] Ti amo. Ti ... well, we gotta talk. We got a lifetime ahead of us, Loose. We gotta find something to say.

LUCE [*Mutters.*] Non mi capisci. Senti ... senti ... perchè non puoi sentire?

CHUCK Come down off your high-class pedestal. You're in Canada now. Halifax. You don't have a big house in Milan and another goddamn mansion on lake whatever and a grandmother with a villa in Florence and ... well –

LUCE [*Mutters.*] Ma, non dev'essere così ... need not to be so ... [LUCE *fantasizes. She sits comfortably curled up, reading a magazine.* CHUCK *enters, gives her a cigarette, perches on the arm of the chair.*]

CHUCK D'you want me to stay around, darling?

LUCE [*No accent.*] Not today, it's been a long day – I just wanna settle down and relax for a while, sleep a bit maybe.

CHUCK [*Ruffling her hair.*] Okay, I won't pressure you.

LUCE Come back when I'm feeling like it and make me laugh.

CHUCK Sure – I got things of my own to do anyway.

LUCE You don't mind if I go down to New York in the morning? I have an audition.

CHUCK Great, need some spondoolix? [*Takes out a fistful of dollars.*]

LUCE No – I have my own money.

CHUCK Well, if I don't see you before you go ... good luck –

LUCE That's what I like most about you, Chuck, you give me room ... you let me breathe and be free ... and whenever I need you ...

[LUCE's *fantasy ends.*]

CHUCK Listen to me, Loose! I take you to live in the Italian part of town, don't I? I find us a room in ... At least you could talk to my papa when he calls, it's not like he doesn't speak Italian.

LUCE He is not Italian.

CHUCK Look ... what d'you want? You want roses? I'll bring you roses ... you want me to carry you away on a white horse? I'll carry you ... I can't even ride a goddamn horse. Want me to stand on my head?

LUCE [*Not watching.*] Is Napolitano. Your papa. Napolitano is not Italian.

[CHUCK *falls in a heap, defeated.*]

CHUCK You're home now, Loose. [LUCE *shrugs, goes back to her magazine.*] You're home. You're just gonna have to get used to it. [*Pauses.*] And nobody here has time to spend a whole week reading one magazine. And sitting in one place. Okay? You just gotta get used to it, that's all.

Scene Eleven

The train, fall, 1945.

DIANA Yes ... this is it. The guard says another couple of minutes. [*Gathers* RUTH's *things together, straightens her fur.*] This is where you have to change trains, Ruthie.

RUTH Maybe I should stay on.

DIANA What?

RUTH Just for another day or two ... as far as Lethbridge. So I can see you off – I could always catch a train back – if I wanted to.

DIANA What a way to talk! Besides, I'm not going to Lethbridge.
We're staying with Paul's father first, near Regina. I told
you, I'm going to see where he grew up.

RUTH You'll come and see me?

DIANA Yes ... and you must come out to us. You and David ...
come for Christmas.

RUTH I'm nearly there and you'll still be on the train. Even
tomorrow when I'm in my house ...
[DIANA *half pushes* RUTH *out of the train.*]

Scene Twelve

Fall, 1945. CHUCK *and* LUCE *are in their room in Halifax.*
DAVE *is at Hamilton Station, and* PAUL *at Regina Station.*
CHUCK *is playing 'Der Fuhrer's Face' in a Spike Jones
imitation. Suddenly he stops, realizing he is not too
brilliant.*

CHUCK Well, I'm just a boy from Halifax – what d'you expect,
Glen Miller? [*Plays another snatch, stops.*] Jesus, the
war's over – that doesn't mean anything any more ...
Loose ... [LUCE *is too far away to hear.*] Loose ... I gotta
find some other songs ... [*Shakes his head, mystified,
picks out the melody of 'Sentimental Journey.'*] Loose ...

DAVE Ruthie ...

PAUL Diana ... can you cook?

CHUCK [*Stops playing.*] You're home, Loose ...

PAUL Canadian style, I mean – Canadian style – can you make
pyrogies?

DAVE Will I recognize you?

PAUL What if it isn't ...

DAVE What if?

PAUL ... like in the letters ... What if ...

DAVE What? ...

CHUCK Loose you're in Canada now!
[CHUCK *begins the melody of 'Sentimental Journey'
again.*]

Scene Thirteen

A seaside promenade, 1941. RUTH *sits on a bench.* DAVE, *wearing his uniform, enters.*

DAVE Anyone sitting here?

RUTH I was waiting on a friend.

DAVE Male or female?

RUTH A girl.

DAVE [*Imitates* RUTH.] A girl? Oh, she can sit on my lap. [*Sits down.*]

RUTH [*Flirtatious.*] Who do you think you are?

DAVE James Michael O'Sullivan. You can call me Dave. [*Holds out his hand.*]

RUTH [*Not taking it.*] Dave ... oh. Not James?

DAVE That's my dad. I chose Dave –

RUTH You christened yourself?

DAVE Yeah ... sure. It's a better name. Tougher. Well, don't you have a name?

RUTH Oh ... Ruthie. Ruth Watson. [DAVE *kisses her hand.* RUTH *withdraws her hand, giggles.*]

RUTH What'd you do that for?

DAVE Haven't you ever met a Canadian? We all kiss hands ... or rub noses.

RUTH You talk funny.

DAVE You don't wanna say that. Last person said that to me I said, 'You wanna talk funny too?' So I broke a few of his teeth. I was real polite about it. Offered to pick them up after. [*Laughs.*]

RUTH Poor man.

DAVE Yeah. Poor knuckles.

RUTH D'you fight a lot?

DAVE Sure. That's what we're here for. [RUTH *grimaces.*] Oh ... I'm putting you on. I never done nothing like that. I been sitting on my knuckles for two years just about. You know, we're the only outfit in military history with a birthrate higher than the deathrate! Wait 'til they let me at them, though. [*Aims his fist.*] Where are you from anyways? You talk funny too.

RUTH Dundee. Scotland ... I joined the land army and came down south.

DAVE You mean you milk cows?

RUTH No. I get put on the hedging mostly ... Sometimes they let me prune. [DAVE *pulls a face.*] What?

DAVE My mom used to feed me those when I couldn't go.

RUTH Not that kind. [*Giggles.*] Pruning. [*Shows him.*]

DAVE Can I buy you a drink?

RUTH What?

DAVE In a pub. [*Nods in direction of pub.*]

RUTH Thanks all the same – I'm listening to the band.

DAVE Oh ... well, in that case ... [*Gets up as if to leave.*]
[RUTH *fantasizes. She is tied to a tree by her hands.*]

RUTH Help me ... help me ... the Indians are going to burn my bones!
[DAVE *becomes part of her fantasy without turning around. He sings the 'Indian Love Call' elongating the words.*]

DAVE [*Singing.*] 'When I'm calling you-ooo-oo-ooo, will you answer true-ooo-oo-oooo?'

RUTH Help, help, help.

DAVE [*He turns, becomes a Mountie and goes into the 'Mountie's Song' riding like a 'pack of angry wolves' chasing some unknown assailant, ready to get his quarry dead or alive. He fires a volley of shots and unties* RUTH.]

RUTH Oh, thank you, thank you.

DAVE Think nothing of it, Ma'am. Just a day in the life of a Mountie. [*Salutes, goes away whistling 'Indian Love Call.'*]

RUTH I think I'm in love.
[RUTH's *fantasy ends.*]

DAVE I should be ... [*Meaning 'pushing on.'*]

RUTH [*Quickly.*] Are you in the army?

DAVE Yeah. I'm a general.

RUTH Well, if you're a general, you can afford to buy me a green goddess – after my friend comes.

DAVE [*Sits down.*] So. Where are you from in Scotland?

RUTH I told you. Dundee.

DAVE That's a cake.

RUTH It's a place.

DAVE Yeah, you're right. It's in Canada.

RUTH You ... [*Hits him in mock frustration.*]

DAVE [*Protecting himself.*] Wrong again – I meant Dundas –
now you're not gonna tell me that's in Scotland too. Last
time I saw it, it was ten miles up the road from where I
live, but they could'a moved it, it's been two years. You
know something? You can drive 'round the world in
Canada – no need to go outside of Ontario – we got a
Paris and a Melbourne and a Delhi ... and a Hamilton,
that's where I'm from.

RUTH Ontario?

DAVE Yeah. That's the best part of Canada.

RUTH Isn't it awful cold there?

DAVE Cold? In summer it gets up over a hundred. We drive
out to the cottage in summer. We got this cottage, see,
on the lake there, and we get the boat out and ... it's up
over a hundred degrees every day.

RUTH A cottage? And a boat?

DAVE Yeah, sure. We drive out there on weekends.

RUTH You got a car?

DAVE Sure. Everyone has a car.
[RUTH *fantasizes. Music: wedding bells, wedding march.*]

RUTH Ruth O'Sullivan. The supper's ready, Davie darling. I'm
just picking some roses to put on the snowy white table
cloth. If they grow any thicker we'll never get through
the door into our cottage.

DAVE Good. I'm starving. I've been hewing wood and drawing
water all day.

RUTH Have you parked the car?

DAVE I left it in the paddock. It's too big for the garage.

RUTH [*Bending over the oven.*] I've roasted that moose you
caught, Davie. [DAVE *bends over and squeezes her.*] Oh,
don't ...

DAVE I can't keep my hands off you. You're the best wife a
man could have.

RUTH [*Turns to him, beaming.*] I'm the happiest person in the
world.

DAVE My woman!
[RUTH'*s fantasy ends.*]

RUTH You must have to work awful hard to have a cottage and
a car and a boat.

DAVE No. You get them for signing up. [*Laughs.*]

RUTH You're pulling my leg.

DAVE Scared it'll come off in my hand? [*Touches her leg.*]
Think it'll stand a dance?

RUTH Where?

DAVE Here.

RUTH On the promenade?

DAVE Aren't you hip to the jive?

RUTH Nobody's dancing. [DAVE *pulls her to her feet.*] Ooooh!
[DAVE *and* RUTH *jitterbug.*]

Scene Fourteen

The train, fall, 1945.

DIANA [*Calling into the corridor.*] Say there ... wake me up at
seven will you? Seven sharp. I don't want to miss Lake
Superior. You won't forget. [*To herself.*] Conductor. I
must get it right, he's a conductor, not a guard.
Incredible accents. Will my children speak like that?
Imagine turning up at the tennis club ... [*Fake American
accent.*] 'Hi, how's it going? Come on, do you wanna hit
a couple of balls around or not?' They'd laugh me off the
court! Must remember not to say 'knock up' – he was
very insistent. Hope I don't have to spend too much
time with his horrible old father. Conductor. Do you tip
in this country? [*Calls out.*] Conductor! You'd better
remember – Lake Superior. Oh, hurry up.

Scene Fifteen

CHUCK *and* LUCE*'s room, Halifax, 1947.* LUCE *is staring
out the window.* CHUCK *enters.*

CHUCK Come away from that window – d'you wanna get killed?
If they break the glass! ... [LUCE *sits down.*] They don't

mean it. Well, it's not against you ... It's against me too. If I catch the sons of ... Look ... I been in two fights today already over you. [*Shows his wounds.*] Don't you care? [*Pushes his hand at her.*] Sangre! [LUCE *stares at him miserably, picks up her rosary. Silence.*] Oh put that thing away. You know you don't go for that stuff. It's gonna kill Mama, you know that? She was so proud when I married you – and now this. Bastards! [*Shakes his fist at the window.*] Well, you could just talk to her couldn't you? What's the matter with you? Why couldn't you have just talked to the neighbours when they came 'round? Who do you think you are anyway?

LUCE   Paisani!

CHUCK   Peasants! It's no wonder they turn on you. It's no wonder our own people call you a fascist and break our windows ...

LUCE   How they know who I am? I not go outside ...

CHUCK   It's *because* you don't go outside. If they got to know you ... If you just talked with them ... Parla, yes? Tell them ... See, they're getting called fascists themselves – fascisti – every day. They're getting attacked and you ... you just stay home and act the lady –

LUCE   [*Interrupts.*] O! ... lascia stare ... lascia stare ...

CHUCK   They figure if anyone 'round here's a fascist it's gonna be you – or me, for bringing you back from Italy. They don't understand!

LUCE   They are Calabresi!

CHUCK   You're a goddamn snob! I suppose you think my father's a peasant. Is everyone from Naples a peasant too?

LUCE   [*Shrugs.*] Che miseria! Che miseria!

CHUCK   Well, at least he stays in touch with me. Not like yours. Ach! Naples, Calabria, spaghetti, baloney, whatever way you slice it, it's still Italy. Italy. You know, before the war my old man had my mother embroider a poem to hang over the bed – "Open my heart and you will see. / 'Graved inside it, Italy." Used to bring people in to look at it, 'til he found out it was written by an Englishman. Took it down. Italy! Goddammit, why couldn't they be on the right side from the start? [*Pause.*] Then we wouldn't have met, right? [LUCE *begins to cry, quietly.*] Oh, Loose,

come on. We got each other, haven't we? You've always got me. It don't matter what they say you are. I know it's not true.
[CHUCK *could have said this with more certainty. He hugs her. She clings to him.*]

Scene Sixteen

PAUL *is waiting for* DIANA *at Regina Station, 1945.*

PAUL Twelve forty-five. They said twelve forty-five. [*Looks at his watch.*] Quarter after ten. I should have coffee, what if it comes in while I'm gone? I wish the old man had a phone. I'd'a called him ...
[*Pause.* PAUL *fantasizes. In his fantasy, he plays alternately himself and his father.*]

PAUL [*As his father.*] Canada is good to you son – you must be good to her. You go and fight. [*As himself.*] The war's over, Papa. If you'd only buy a radio you'd ... [*As his father.*] Over? Thank God. [*As himself.*] Papa ... I want you to meet Diana Manning – Sorry Tomachuk – must get it right – my wife – your name, my wife. Wife. [*As his father.*] O moy ridna donichka. Tea ya krasna te shoa ya hotchu ...* [*As himself.*] Okay, okay, she's my wife, not yours! [*As his father.*] O, moya donichka. [*Weeps.* PAUL'*s fantasy ends. He is back at the station.*] Maybe we should just go straight to Lethbridge. The way he eats! He'll probably fart at the table! Say's he's taught the dog to bark in Ukrainian. Jeez!

* *Translation: Oh my darling little daughter, you're exactly what I wanted ...*

Scene Seventeen

The train, fall, 1945. LUCE *is in her room, Halifax, alone on the couch, nursing her rosary.*

DIANA [*Drying her eyes.*] I'm such an idiot, Paul. I've cried half the journey ... Whatever will you think of me? Enough to flood Lake Superior. I know you told me it was the biggest lake in the world, but I just thought you were boasting. Oh, I do love you. You're such an extraordinary person, so single-minded. I really admire that. I'll help you to be a great writer. I should be writing everything down for you. I've forgotten so much already. It's so easy to forget. Things – even the most traumatic – places ... faces ... Winnipeg? Oh, we've got five hours here. [*Gets up and leaves the train.*]

LUCE Mama. Mama. Mama.

Scene Eighteen

Hamilton Station, fall, 1945. DAVE *is still waiting for* RUTH.

DAVE I'll give her another hour ... That train can't be that late ... [*Takes a folded pin-up from his breast pocket, looks at it lovingly.*] You better not let me down, Rita, you saw me through before, you better not let me down now. Well, we've been together for six years, haven't we?
[DAVE *fantasizes. Music, 'Put the Blame on Me.'* RUTH *comes on. She has become Rita Hayworth. She comes straight to him. A dramatic embrace.*]

DAVE [*Murmurs.*] Rita. Rita Hayworth.

RITA What a war you had, James!

DAVE I've had a few stories to tell since I got back.

RITA They'll never really know what you went through.

DAVE Me – ah, come on – all I did was drive a truck.

RITA Men would've died without supplies.

DAVE [*Cocky.*] Spent half the war in the lockup. [*Laughs.*] I'd fight for my girl anytime.

RITA Tiger! You can't keep those fists to yourself, can you?

DAVE Keeping us sitting around in the Limey mud for three years. We weren't over there to sit on our knuckles.

RITA Oh Dave! [*Throws herself on him.*]

DAVE [*Stopping her.*] You're still a virgin?

RITA Of course.

DAVE I'd leave you standing here – you know that? I don't go in no place where other men've been before.

RITA Come on. I can't wait any longer.

DAVE Not here – wait a minute.

RITA Behind the train.

DAVE But it's gonna move any minute.

RITA Who cares?

DAVE I love you, Rita. [*Stands staring straight ahead.*]

Scene Nineteen

An Italian café, 1944. There should be a map of Italy on the wall. CHUCK *is at a piano. He plays 'Sentimental Journey.'* DIANA *is on the train, fall, 1946. During* DIANA's *speech,* LUCE *enters the café, and, standing, sips espresso.*

DIANA Well, that was Winnipeg, Paul. Thank goodness we won't be living there – Lethbridge will be much nicer. Maybe I didn't see the right bit – you'll have to show it to me. I looked for Portage and Main but I couldn't find it, so I sat on a wall and ate oranges like a tramp. Oh Paul, I'm almost in your court – it's as if you were sitting right there. [*Across from her.*] It's been so long – I can only think of you in your uniform – what will you be wearing? Grey flannels and a nice cravat? And that fairisle pullover mummy knitted you for Christmas? [*Looks out the window.*] Portage la Prairie, Carberry, Brandon, Verdun ...
[*Action changes to the café. At the piano,* CHUCK *has changed the melody to 'It's a Long Way to Tipperary.' He is drinking brandy.*]

63

CHUCK [*Calls out.*] Fingers stiff as triggers. [LUCE *pretends not to hear him.*] Not done, eh? Playing on the management's instrument. Well, you tell them I been playing soldiers all this last year just so they could keep this place open. [*Tries out a few more notes of 'Tipperary.'*] You know, the last time I played? In a church in Ortona – honest – the Tin Hats were in town. You know them? Bunch of Canadians – great entertainers when they're sober. I got to play with them – listen. [*Plays 'O sole mio,' taking the romance out of it.*]

LUCE No, no, no. [*Laughs.*]

CHUCK You can do better?

[LUCE *shakes her head.*]

CHUCK O sole mio. Italian for you are my sunshine – know the words? Come on, sing.

LUCE [*Tongue-tied.*] Is for man to sing. Is man's song.

CHUCK Oh ... you talk English? Well, teach it to me then ... come on, I'll sing it ... [*Offers to let her sit down.*] [LUCE *refuses the offer, shyly.*] Oh, it's okay – my dad's Italian, Malecarne, that's me – bad meat – that's what it means, doesn't it? Malecarne. [LUCE *laughs.*] Musta been lousy butchers when they were over here, that's why they came to Canada – see, over there they can't tell the difference! [*Laughs.*] See, not all of us Italians throw in the towel. Some of us keep fighting. [*Holds out his hand.*] Chuck.

LUCE Luce.

CHUCK Come again? Here, write that down. [*Holds out a napkin for her to write on.*] Oh – Loose.

LUCE Loo-chay.

CHUCK [*Writing.*] Chuck – Charles – see – Carlo. Carlo and Loose. [*Draws a heart.*] Heart. [*Pats his heart.*]

LUCE Cuore.

CHUCK Cuore. [*Pause.*] Bella ragazza. [*Kisses his fingers Italian style.*] Here – [*Pats the stool beside him.*] [LUCE *wants to sit, but does not.*] You know the last time I was in Florence? About three months ago. Bang, bang, bang ... [CHUCK *acts out snipers for* LUCE*'s benefit.* LUCE *nods.*] Italians – not Krauts – snipers – trying to get us – ungrateful bastards, goddammit ... All my life I been thinking of the time when I'd come to Italy and when I get here – [*Drinks.*] it does nothing but rain.

LUCE Tocca. –

CHUCK I am talking. Here – here, look – Canadian, that's me. [*Traces the campaign route up from Sicily on the map.*] We liberate you, right? Sicily, see, Potenza, Maple Leaf City.... I was about here when your side threw in the towel – Ortona – you heard about Ortona? I won't forget Ortona. Florence, Rimini. This is my second time around in Florence, and it's still raining.

LUCE Tocca. [*Shows him that she means 'play.'*]

CHUCK Come on, sing.

LUCE [*Smiles, suddenly sings out in a clear, tuneful voice.*] O mio babbino caro, / Mi piace bello bello –

CHUCK [*Listens, amazed, then grabs her.*] Hey, siddown!

LUCE [*Sits.*] I will to be cantatrice. [*Pause.*] Sing.

CHUCK You don't say? Hey, we'll sing together – we'll get the Tin Hats to take us on ... Why not? [*Clowns, a bit drunk, sings.*] Hitler, has only got one ball; / Goering has two but they are small; / Himmler, has something sim'lar; And poor Goebbels has no balls at all! [LUCE *laughs, delighted.*] I go see your papa, yes? Some kinda crazy man letting you out on the street when the Canadians are in town, Loose. Know where Canada is? Canada ... me ...

LUCE America.

CHUCK America? That's on the outskirts of Halifax, isn't it?

LUCE Yes? You Yank?

CHUCK Canada's where it's happening. You better believe it. I'll show it to you, listen, I'll go and see your papa. Listen – you're gonna sing. You better do it over there. No one does it, see – over here you got competition – over there they all got frost on the lung. [*Coughs.*]

LUCE Canada. [*Pause.*] Suona, Canada.

CHUCK So you'll come? The one I asked in Ortona slapped my face – she thought I was after something else. [*Winks.*] You know what my old man says – papa? 'You marry nice Italian girl, Carlo, you never have to clean your own shoes again.' I laughed at him, 'til I got sent over here and found out what mud was. [*He shows her his dirty boots,* LUCE *laughs. He puts his arm around* LUCE.] I like you, you know that? You've got a sense of humour. I like that. You're a nice quiet girl, with a sense of humour. You're a beautiful girl, you know that?

LUCE   I sing. [LUCE *hums the tune of 'I'll Never Smile Again.'* CHUCK *picks the tune out. She sings a parrotted version, not understanding the words.* CHUCK *fantasizes. Big band swells.* CHUCK *is in the spotlight conducting.* LUCE *stands shyly in the background, singing.* CHUCK'*s fantasy ends.* LUCE *sings the last line of the song, stops suddenly, and smiles.*] I learn radio.

CHUCK   Very good. Listen ... you know this? ... [*Plays the first line of 'You Are My Sunshine' and sings it.*] Go on, you. Yes, you.

LUCE   [*Pointing to herself.*] You –

CHUCK   You are my sunshine.

LUCE   You are mine ... sun ...

CHUCK   Shine. My only sunshine. Solo sunshine. Here, we'll make a duo ... You make me happy, when skies are grey.

LUCE   Felice.

CHUCK   Felice. [*They laugh.*] Molto felice.

LUCE   Mister Canada. Canada. [CHUCK *hugs* LUCE. *She jumps up.*] I must to go. Is not allowed I am here.

CHUCK   Here – wait a minute. You got five days to try me on for size. That's how long my leave lasts.
[CHUCK *takes* LUCE *in his arms and kisses her. They remain like this until the end of Act One.*]

Scene Twenty

A field, 1943. DAVE *and* RUTH *wander on to have a picnic.* RUTH *has a basket.*

RUTH   It was terrible. I thought you'd stood me up. I went a bit crazy – I ran away from the farm – I don't know where I thought I was going – home most likely – I stole an old lady's knickers off a clothesline.

DAVE   [*Laughs.*] If I'd known that when I was inside I'd've felt a whole lot better.

RUTH   I thought they'd sent you to Dieppe.

DAVE Didn't even know it was happening. I was in the lockup like I told you.

RUTH I went to your base – they said they'd never heard of you.

DAVE They wished they hadn't.

RUTH Then I got arrested by this sourpuss policewoman. She was asking what you were like. I told her you looked like Cary Grant – she wanted to meet you –

DAVE Yeah? What's she look like?

RUTH Oh ... she was about eighty. Do you know Dave. Jenny Dodds is getting married.

DAVE Let's sit down.

RUTH You know about her – she's on the farm. That makes five of them married and two widows. There's only me and Mary Meadows left and she never washes herself.

DAVE You wanna be a widow?

RUTH No ... but it's better than being on the shelf. They all say it's easier to catch another one if you've already had one.

DAVE Is that what they say?

RUTH Jenny Dodds's got an uncle in Canada. She says it's lovely there – there isn't even a war on. [DAVE *looks around, a bit restless.*] Don't you like it here?

DAVE Yeah. You can see the sea.

RUTH She wishes her Mick was a Canadian. I borrowed an egg from the farm ... oh, and I swapped my wellingtons for some butter coupons, so it's real butter on the bread. Who needs boots in summer anyway?

DAVE Hmmmm?

RUTH Are there places like this in Canada? ...

DAVE No. We don't have the sea – I like the smell.

RUTH D'you miss it? Canada?

DAVE Sure.

RUTH What do you miss?

DAVE I dunno. The bush maybe. There's a kinda quiet there – down on the Indian trail, yeah. You can hear the animals moving around, you know ... like cracking the twigs and moving their jaws, yeah ... and you can hear the fish jump, out at the lake, and when the ducks fly out over the water ... [*Lapses into silence.*]

RUTH What do you do?

DAVE [*Laughs suddenly.*] Shoot 'em. [*Fires.*]

RUTH Don't!

DAVE I go hunting sometimes.

RUTH Do you shoot the animals? Like the sassenachs do when they come up to Scotland?

DAVE Sure. Everyone does ...

RUTH Everyone?

DAVE Sure. Or sometimes you can go down the store and get meat for nothing.

RUTH Free?

DAVE Well ... I mean ... you don't have to shoot it. You can buy as much as you like.

RUTH It sounds wonderful.

DAVE Would you? ... Would you mind if I kissed you?

RUTH How come you asked?

[DAVE *kisses* RUTH *very gently. She wants to continue. He pulls back.*]

DAVE Loose lips sink ships. That means you don't kiss in public. [*Pause.*] Can't we go someplace more private?

RUTH This is private.

DAVE There might be someone watching.

RUTH It doesn't matter. We do it in the streets ... at the bus stop ...

DAVE You? ...

RUTH [*Hastily.*] Well, not me.

DAVE I ... I think I respect you. [*Pause.*] What's that on your face?

RUTH [*Embarrassed*] Powder. Why? Don't you like it?

DAVE It smells.

RUTH Oh, I'll take it off. [*Licks her handkerchief and washes her face.*]' Is that better? [*Offers him her cheeks.*]

DAVE [*Not accepting the offer.*] I don't like that stuff. [*Long silence.*] You should be able to be with someone and not have to say anything. [*Pause.*] I feel like I want to spend all my time with you. [*Pause.*] Do you think we're lovers?

RUTH Do you?

DAVE Hey, come on. [*Drags her to her feet.*] Dance ...

RUTH Here?

DAVE Why not? You said there wasn't anybody looking –

Scene Twenty

RUTH All right.
    [*They dance.*]
DAVE Ruthie ... I like you better than anyone I ever liked
    before. [RUTH *gazes at him, waiting.*] Do you like
    Canada?
RUTH I don't know.
DAVE Do you want to go? [RUTH *looks at him.*] With me? Like
    ... do you wanna get married or something?
RUTH Oh Dave ...
    [*They kiss. They remain like this until the end of Act
    One.*]

Scene Twenty-One

*PAUL and DIANA are facing each other again at the same
English café three years later, in early 1944.*

PAUL Smoke?
DIANA No thanks. You didn't smoke before did you?
PAUL Beats chewing your fingers. So. How's the police?
DIANA Oh fine ... fine. The American soldiers are a bit of a pain
    in the neck. They're so ... boisterous. But I'm getting
    used to people having nervous breakdowns all over the
    place – it'll be fine as long as no one drops a bomb on
    my head. D'you still go to bed with Karl Marx under
    your pillow?
PAUL Marx?
DIANA I thought you were a comm –
PAUL Oh, that.
DIANA Well?
PAUL Sure. [*He is not sure.*]
DIANA I met a Fabian last month. He'd been beaten up. He was
    a conscientious objector – but of course that's not the
    same thing, is it?
PAUL I volunteered.
DIANA I'm glad. [*Takes his hand.*]
PAUL I guess I was just a kid. You gotta believe in something,
    isn't that right? [*Pause.*] Did you think about me?
DIANA When?

PAUL Any time.

DIANA I was going out with an Australian for a while. My father hated him.

PAUL Did you eat the chocolate?

DIANA What chocolate?

PAUL I gave it to you.

DIANA That was two years ago.

PAUL I've been thinking about you.

DIANA Me?

PAUL When we got posted back here I just hung around all the police stations figuring I'd meet you.

DIANA It's a wonder you weren't arrested.

PAUL I was careful.

DIANA Why me? You must've met dozens of girls.

PAUL I figured I ... I owed you an apology.

DIANA What for?

PAUL I insulted you. I don't go 'round insulting women. I'm sorry.

DIANA What did you say?

PAUL I said you were English.
       [DIANA *erupts in a peal of laugher, then stops, realizing* PAUL *is serious.*]

DIANA Oh ... it's forgotten.

PAUL Will you marry me?

DIANA What?

PAUL We'll be in France next week.

DIANA What did you say?

PAUL Well will you? ... I won't guarantee I'll stay alive ... but if I do I'm gonna make things happen. This war's opened everything up, you must see that? Well?

DIANA Oh, you're such a ... [*Pause.*] You're not serious? [*Pause.*] What a hoot. [*Pause.*] What can I say?

PAUL Yes.

DIANA I'm stunned. I mean ... you don't know a thing about me.

PAUL We can write. It's been done before.

DIANA My parents ... you don't know them.

PAUL So? What is there to know about them? I've just been thinking about you all the time. I think of you every night ...

DIANA My father's going to be mayor next year – he's a captain
in the home guard. My brother Hugh's a squadron
leader – I don't think they'd find you very – suitable.
Neither would you.

PAUL What's that got to do with anything?

DIANA Well if they were to meet you –

PAUL Fine, when do you want me to come over?

DIANA Oh Paul, you're so incredibly serious. It's so funny ...
[PAUL *looks down into his lap, distraught.*] Look ... I don't
know how I feel about you – I'm totally confused, I
mean – out of the blue – I mean it's very flattering, but ...

PAUL Don't you want to get married?

DIANA I didn't say that but ... I don't know you –

PAUL Yes you do, we've known each other for two years. I'm
an okay person – I'm as good as any Australian. I don't
want to go overseas without ... without something to
come back to –

DIANA But you'll go back to Canada.

PAUL We can go together.

DIANA Canada? Oh, I've never even considered – I mean,
whatever would my parents say? Not that it's any
business of theirs. You are a hoot.

PAUL I've been writing – I've written a lot of poetry since – I've
never shown it to anyone. I write about home a lot. It's
the greatest country on earth – after England of course.
I've written about you.

DIANA Paul, I ...

PAUL I'll wait outside the police station every night. I'll go
AWOL.

DIANA No ... I have to think.

PAUL You don't – there's no time for that.

DIANA But Paul, I ...

PAUL Please. Didn't I say please?

DIANA You don't just ask somebody something like that, out of
the blue, and expect an answer.

PAUL I'll keep asking it. I'll keep asking you 'til you say yes.
Listen – 'The eternal in woman draws us on ...'

DIANA Das Ewig-Weibliche, Zieht uns hinan.

PAUL [*Shouts, joyfully.*] You see ... it's meant to be. It's –

DIANA Sssh! We studied Goethe for matric, that's all.

PAUL I love you Diana.

DIANA I can't. You don't understand. They'd never forgive me. My parents ... I could never come back here.

[PAUL *gets up suddenly and kisses* DIANA *full on the lips. All three couples are now happily in each other's arms.*]

72

Act II, Scene One

Hamilton Station, 1945. RUTH *is searching for* DAVE *on the crowded platform. She carries a bunch of flowers.*

RUTH Yoo-hoo! [*She spots* DAVE, *puts her carry-cot and bag down, and rushes over to him.*]

DAVE Hey! [*Pause. They look at each other, then hug.*]

RUTH I thought you weren't here.

DAVE Would I not be here?

RUTH Oh Dave. [*They hug. He is squashing the flowers.*] Mind ... Someone gave them to me ... Oh, it's all right, everyone's getting them – over there, look, by the train. You look ... different without your uniform. [*Lies.*] I like your hat.

DAVE You're looking ...

RUTH I've put on a bit of weight.

DAVE Have you?

RUTH You noticed, didn't you?

DAVE Well, it's kinda ... noticeable. [*Looking at her fur.*] Where'd you trap the rat?

RUTH It's not a rat, Dave. It's real.

DAVE Hm. It's a wonder they let you in with it. It's probably got rabies. [*Pretends that it bites him, clowns.*]

RUTH Rita's right behind you. [DAVE *jumps around.*] No ... there – [*Gestures to the carry-cot.*]

DAVE Rita?

RUTH That's her name. I told you – well don't you still like Rita Hayworth?

DAVE Who's she?

RUTH Oh Dave. Go on. Pick her up.

DAVE [*Not touching the baby.*] Yeah but ... we promised to call it after my mom.

RUTH Who did?

DAVE Cissy. I told you ... you can call her Rita for a second name if you like, but my mom ...

RUTH Cissy Rita?

DAVE Well, just Cissy then.

RUTH No, it's awful. It's not even a real name.

DAVE It's my mom's name.

RUTH It's what you call people who're a bit soft.

DAVE You don't know anything. [*Pause.*] Well, it's not asking
much is it? [*Pause.*] Your eyes are red. [*Bends down.*]
Hello Cissy.
[RUTH *gets out her powder compact and dabs at her face.*
DAVE *watches her.*]

RUTH You don't mind?

DAVE No ... that's good.

RUTH Do I look all right?

DAVE Yeah ... I mean, you just came from the war and all that,
didn't you?

RUTH Aren't you happy?

DAVE Yeah ... but it takes a little while to get used to it.

RUTH But you've been married a while. [DAVE *stares at* RUTH.]
You're going to look after us aren't you?

DAVE What kinda question is that?

RUTH I'm sorry about your dad, Dave. [DAVE *shrugs, unable to
say anything.*] Are we going to stand here all day?

DAVE There's a little problem, see ... Here's the situation – we
haven't got our house yet. Oh don't worry, we'll get it.
We'll live at my mother's house ... I've got a couple of
handles on a job at Stelco – something should come
through any time.

RUTH But you said in your letter –

DAVE I know. We're just gonna stay a little while. My mom's
put her double bed in my room – we can keep the baby
by the bed. But we all have to be quiet. None of that
grunting or groaning or anything – see, there's my
brother Tom in the next room ... and she has to get up
in the morning to cook our breakfast –

RUTH I'll do that.

DAVE Yeah. Well ...
[RUTH *picks up the baby.* DAVE *takes the bag. She offers
him the flowers, but he refuses to carry them.*]

RUTH I might call her Rita by mistake sometimes.

DAVE Don't do that. I mean ... she's been through a lot ...
wondering if I was gonna get killed and all ... then losing
my dad.

RUTH [*Looking at the baby.*] You do like her, don't you?

Scene Three

DAVE Its only since my dad died ... Come on –

RUTH She said ... [DAVE *grabs her and picks her up.* RUTH *screams, delighted.*] You'll put your back out.

DAVE Takes more than a sack of Quaker Oats to do that.

RUTH Dave!

DAVE I don't want no more of this squawkin, okay? Wife!
[RUTH *beats on him in a futile attempt to escape, enjoying the chance to bellow, laughing as he carries her out.*]

Scene Four

CHUCK *and* LUCE's *room, Halifax, 1948.* LUCE *sits in the chair, painting her toenails.* CHUCK *enters.*

CHUCK So, how'd it go?

LUCE Okay.

CHUCK Did they like you?

LUCE Sure.

CHUCK 'Course they liked you. The old guys don't get too many classy Italian ladies coming in to sing to them for free.

LUCE Many are deaf. Sordo, yes?

CHUCK 'Course they are. You'll probably be deaf when you're eighty. But they liked you, eh? That's the main thing. Bravo. Did they ask you to come back?

LUCE Next week.

CHUCK So you're going?

LUCE I guess.

CHUCK I guess ... Then I guess I'll come along too and play for you, how's that? If we can't do it for money, we'll do it for love, or humanity or whatever you wanna call it. Oh, I forgot. Present from papa. [*Gives it to her.*]

LUCE Pizza!

CHUCK Okay. You don't have to eat it – he's got customers lining up ...

LUCE Ach! [*Puts her nail polish aside, picks up a magazine and buries herself in it.*]

CHUCK You know what? He put his finger on a need. People need pizza. That's what North America's all about,

79

Loose. He's sitting on a small fortune. You find a need and you fill it and you make a pile of dough. That's capitalism. [*Pause.*] And you need me. [*Takes the magazine away from her.*] He loves you like a daughter. Well, he's real sorry your folks don't stay in touch. He wants to change that – pay for them to come over here. [LUCE *snorts, returns to her magazine.*] Okay, so they've got a few bucks. It don't mean that we're peasants. And now that I got you singing again ... I got you going out. Well, they've stopped calling us fascists. I told you they would, didn't I? It's gonna be all right, Loose. Trust me, everything's gonna be – [CHUCK *attempts to put his arm around* LUCE. *She screams.*] So what do you want? Tell me that?

LUCE   I want ... I want make something. I want work.

CHUCK   Oh, come on, Loose. Just be patient, eh? There aren't jobs for the guys. Why don't you just settle down? [CHUCK *fantasizes.* LUCE *is sewing a sampler.*] Come on let's see.

LUCE   No ... no, is a surprise.

CHUCK   Come on, what's it say? [*Peers over her shoulder and reads.*] There's no place like –

LUCE   Oh, Chuck!

CHUCK   Like what ... like Milan, like Florence?

LUCE   Guess again.

CHUCK   You're fantastic – you know that? [LUCE *tosses the sampler aside and jumps into his arms.* CHUCK's *fantasy ends.*] You got a nice place to live here haven't you? [LUCE *goes back to doing her nails.*] C'mon, smile, Loose. [LUCE *smiles obligingly.*] We won't be in one room forever. Put that thing down. You're getting to like it here – it's gonna take time to admit it, that's all. [CHUCK *sits beside her, caresses her, nibbles her ear.*]

LUCE   No!

CHUCK   You like me – you love me, eh, Loose?

LUCE   Si. Sure.

CHUCK   Well, that's what matters. If a guy's wife doesn't love him, then who does? I mean, I coulda married some girl from Halifax who didn't love me, isn't that right? [*Pause.*] Let's make a baby tonight.

Scene Four

LUCE No.

CHUCK Well, now then. [*Grabs her.*]

LUCE Is not room for cat here.

CHUCK You do love me? Go on – say it, say it.

LUCE [*Protects her nail polish.*] Sei molto caro, Chuck. Carino.

CHUCK I love you ... go on ... I wanna hear it in English.

LUCE How many times?

CHUCK Write it out fifty times after school! Listen, me and a couple of guys I went to high school with, we're gonna put a combo together. We'll cut a record ... [LUCE *continues to paint her nails.*] You'll see – it won't be too long. You won't have to spend a lifetime in here painting your goddamn toes!

[LUCE *stays onstage.*]

Scene Five

RUTH *and* DAVE*'s kitchen, Hamilton, 1949.* RUTH *is knitting, a pile of children's toques and mitts beside her. She has made some effort with her appearance, looking forward to* DAVE *coming home.*

RUTH You know what the trouble with this country is? You spend all summer getting ready for winter.

DAVE [*Laughs, jams a child's toque on his head.*] Cheer up, Christmas is coming. [RUTH *snatches the toque.*] Look, I got some cigarette cards for Jamie.

RUTH For Jamie?

DAVE Well, you don't want them, do you?

RUTH He's too young for cigarette cards. He'll eat them. [*Pause.*] It's the fifteenth of August, Dave. [RUTH *fantasizes.* DAVE *produces a huge box of chocolates, gift wrapped.* RUTH *opens them, reacts ecstatically, tries to decide which one to eat.*]

DAVE [*Picking one out.*] Open the stable, here comes the horse – one horse, two horses, three horses, and here's the wild one ... [*Crams chocolates into her mouth.*]

RUTH Oh, Dave, stop it! Stop it! [*Splutters and laughs.*] [RUTH*'s fantasy ends.*]

81

DAVE Yeah, Two days to payday.

RUTH There's a cake in there. She baked it. I presume it's for
you. She wouldn't let me in the kitchen this morning.

DAVE Where is it? I'm starving.

RUTH On the sideboard. [*Nods to inner room.*] It says 'Happy
Anniversary to my son and his wife' in blue writing.

DAVE Why didn't she remind me?

RUTH Maybe she thought you wouldn't need it. [*Pause.*] I got
us one as well.

DAVE Two? We don't need two.

RUTH Mine's got cream in it. Your favourite.

DAVE Let me at them. [*Begins to leave room.*] Hey ... you can't
have any. You gotta lose weight so I can get you one of
those strapless gowns and take you out on the town.
The New Looks, eh? [*Leaves.*]

RUTH [*Sits for a moment, looking after him.*] Lose weight? You
try losing weight when you're always pregnant. [*To the
door through which he left.*] You don't have a girlfriend,
do you Dave? Dave?
[RUTH *stays onstage.*]

Scene Six

The farm in Alberta, 1947. DIANA *is fixing a farm
implement with dogged determination and not much
flair.* PAUL *enters.*

PAUL You could leave that you know.

DIANA [*Automatically.*] It has to be done.

PAUL Do it tomorrow. Let's go bowling. I gotta practise up for
that tournament.

DIANA You haven't got a hope.

PAUL You'll see, I'll get down there every night.

DIANA I wanted to clean the truck tonight. I haven't had time
to – we can't all sit around *dreaming* of the perfect farm.
Somebody has to do the work!

PAUL You're doing great. Just great. But you're too serious ...
[*Puts his arm around her.*]

DIANA There are only twenty-four hours in the day, Paul!

Scene Six

PAUL Yeah, and don't let's make more than half of them for work, eh? [*Pats her reassuringly, begins to leave.*]

DIANA Don't go bowling tonight. [PAUL *leaves.*] You do still love me, Paul? Paul?

RUTH You're not going out with someone else are you, Dave?

DIANA The edge of the world. The edge ... [*Buries her face in her hands.*]

RUTH Don't leave me on my own.

LUCE Why must I always be waiting? That is not why I came here. To wait.

Scene Seven

CHUCK *is in his apartment, Halifax, 1950. He is alone, practising 'The Tennessee Waltz,' with guitar accompaniment, imitating a crooner. He stops.*

CHUCK They don't understand nothing here – none of them ever fought in a war. Bunch of desk cases. I'm sick of just getting to play the legions. I'm gonna make people see what we went through, then they'll have to hire me. I'm gonna drop a bomb on them, sure ...
[CHUCK *continues to practise.*]

Scene Eight

The farm in Alberta, 1950. DIANA *is pulling on her rubber boots, preparing to go outside.*

PAUL Shall I go alone? [DIANA *does not reply.*] Betty and Brian need some advice – they asked me.

DIANA I have too much to do here. Besides we don't talk the same language. [PAUL *makes a dismissive motion.*] I feel as though they're laughing behind my back.

PAUL Brian thinks you're pretty. He told me so.

DIANA He told me too.

PAUL Good.

DIANA Strangers don't tell you things like that – not to your face.

PAUL   Ah, behind your back, eh?

DIANA   *You* don't tell me.

PAUL   Yes I do – tea dusza krasna.

DIANA   I mean in English, you chump! Oh Paul, they laugh at you too, d'you know that? They're all sniggering at us. I see enough of those people at those dreadful socials.

PAUL   Well, you drag us there.

DIANA   We have to make some kind of showing in the community.

PAUL   Showing? What kind of showing do you make? You never even change your clothes.

DIANA   Oh, I see. You want me to primp myself up like the rest of them in their pre-war monuments to bad taste!

PAUL   They think it's you that doesn't have any style.

DIANA   Me? They've got their nerve!

PAUL   Well, why don't you get your hair done?

DIANA   If you wanted a fashion plate you shouldn't've plonked me down near Lethbridge. Have you ever looked in those shops?

PAUL   I just want them to see that you're ... Well, everyone else managed to look –

DIANA   Everyone else? What do they know? If only somebody had a sense of humour! They're not even interested in local politics, in getting anything done. They seem to expect to suffer.

PAUL   If you'd been through the depression and the war –

DIANA   Where do you think I was? [*Pause.*] Can't they put a good face on it instead of laughing at us?

PAUL   They don't laugh.

DIANA   They don't? ... At you and your experiments? ...

PAUL   You have to experiment ... that's how you learn.

DIANA   Don't tell me, tell them. Maybe they've got a point. Maybe you only learn by repeating the old ways.

PAUL   [*Overlapping her line, not listening.*] You've got to try new things. This is a new land. If calls for innovative methods – well of course you believe that.

DIANA   Yes. Yes ... I'm just tired, that's all. I just wonder if it's worth it all.

PAUL   If you don't believe in it, then ...

DIANA   Paul. [*Pause.*] Paul, I want to ask you something.

Scene Eight

PAUL They're worse than the old man. No confidence, no ideas.

DIANA Paul, I think we should adopt a child. [*Pause.*] Are you listening? [PAUL *shakes his head.*] I've already made enquiries.

PAUL Jesus! Can't you wait?

DIANA If we don't then I ... [*Pause.*] I don't see much point in slaving like this.

PAUL We'll have kids of our own ... later. When we're ready.

DIANA You know that's impossible.

PAUL It's not. Nothing's impossible. Nothing.

DIANA They're coming to see us tomorrow.

PAUL I'm going to Lethbridge tomorrow.

DIANA You'd better be here, that's all. You'd better be here.

Scene Nine

DAVE *and* RUTH's *kitchen, Hamilton, 1951.*

RUTH I went to Gallagher's this morning. He was real nice, the young man in there.

DAVE Shhh!

RUTH I won't shhh! [DAVE *glances nervously at the inner room.*] [*Loudly.*] She's listening anyway – and if we whisper ... [*To door.*] Aren't you?

DAVE Okay, that's it. [*Shuts his mouth.*]

RUTH Well, if you don't want to talk about it. [DAVE *motions her to go ahead with a sweeping gesture.*] He said I'd be better to fly. [*Waits for this to sink in.*] In an aeroplane. [DAVE *doesn't reply.*] You don't have to pay for kids under three. I thought maybe we could find a bit extra and I could take all four of them ... Oh, I wish you could come too, Dave. Wouldn't she lend us the ... [*Nods to inner room.*] They fly to Prestwick and we can get the train to Dundee – he'll write all the tickets here – we don't have to bother with anything, isn't that wonderful? Well, I know you've been wanting to go on an aeroplane. My dad wants to take you down to the pub – they've got

85

a snooker table now. I'll bet he never gets home 'til closing. You can help him on his allotment, Angus doesn't lift a finger, just takes all the veges home to Mary and the kids. Well, you read the letter ... Dave ...

DAVE   Look ... [*Keeping his voice down.*] I don't want you going over there.

RUTH   Why not?

DAVE   I don't that's all – not without me.

RUTH   Why not? [DAVE *doesn't reply.*] Well, I don't want to go without you, you know that. [*Pause.*] Are you scared, Dave? Are you scared I wouldn't come back?

DAVE   Shhh!

RUTH   You know I'd come back. You don't have to be scared. Oh, Dave ...

DAVE   You're not going, that's all.

RUTH   It's my money. I filled the coupon in. I thought up the slogan.

DAVE   I gave you the stamp.

RUTH   I bought the marmalade.

DAVE   Whose money paid for it?

RUTH   Mine. What's yours is mine.

DAVE   Okay, so you can have half the Chevy.

RUTH   What Chevy?

DAVE   The one I put the down payment on with the prize money.

RUTH   Oh Dave, you didn't.

DAVE   Take delivery a week Tuesday. Tuesday night we can drive down to Niagara Falls.

RUTH   I ... I don't understand.

DAVE   You don't wanna come?

RUTH   No ... no, I don't.

DAVE   Okay, so I'll take someone else. [*Glances at door.*] She hasn't rode in a car since Edith Jamieson died. [*Waits for an answer from his mother.*] Isn't that right?

RUTH   But Dave. You always said I could take a trip when we had the money.

DAVE   Well, I'm still saying it, but we don't have the money right now. Well, what's the matter – I thought you wanted a car.

RUTH   I can't drive.

Scene Nine

DAVE So? I'll drive.

RUTH It won't even be paid for. You know I don't like the hire purchase.

DAVE Ah c'mon. You're not in Scotland now. This way we can have an extra half hour in bed in the morning. I won't have to take the bus.

RUTH But I'll still have to get up for the kids. Does she know? Was she in on this? [*Raising her voice.*] She encouraged you didn't she? Told you it was your right. Her and her bloody rights.

DAVE Keep it down!

RUTH I'll bet she thinks she's won. Well she hasn't. I'm still going to Scotland and half of that car's mine.

DAVE Which half?

RUTH The bit in the middle where you sit. She can ride in the boot.

[*DAVE laughs. RUTH storms out. DAVE remains onstage through the beginning of the next scene.*]

Scene Ten

CHUCK *and* LUCE's *apartment, Halifax, 1951. A pile of magazines is on the floor.* LUCE *is vacuuming with an old-fashioned vacuum cleaner which is not plugged in. She goes over and over the same spot, concentrating. She is singing to herself.*

DAVE Doesn't know when she's well off. [*Exits.*]

CHUCK Well, it'll be better when we get a couple of carpets. I'm gonna fill all these rooms with furniture for you. None of your utility stuff ...

[LUCE *stops singing.* CHUCK *jumps up and plugs the vacuum in.* LUCE *lets go of the vacuum, putting her hands over her ears.*]

LUCE Too much noise.

CHUCK Look, you do it like this. [CHUCK *shows* LUCE *how to vacuum.* LUCE *turns her back.* CHUCK *laughs and unplugs the vacuum.*] Okay, have it your own way. Who wants a clean house, anyway? Hey, listen, I talked to papa. He

might be needing some extra help – well, you're gonna
have to help pay the rent. It was you that wanted this
place. What's the point of winning a couple of talent
competitions? Where does that get you? We need some
money ...
[LUCE *switches on the vacuum cleaner.* CHUCK *yanks the cord out.*]

LUCE You want clean?

CHUCK I could kill you!

LUCE Come ...
[LUCE *invites* CHUCK *to do so.* CHUCK *relaxes suddenly, laughs.* LUCE *laughs.* CHUCK *hugs her.*]

CHUCK I love you and I don't know why. [*Turns away, picks up a scrapbook.*] Is this how you spend your time while I'm out looking for work? Barbara Ann Scott, eh? [*Whistles.* LUCE *tries to take the book away.*] Judy Garland – not bad ... Lotte Lenya? Marlene Dietrich? They're Germans – bunch of spies.

LUCE No ... they are women. They are success.

CHUCK Krauts aren't women.

LUCE At least they are not in chains.

CHUCK Well, zey should be.
[CHUCK *does a Nazi salute.* LUCE *throws the books at him.* CHUCK *starts to laugh.*]

LUCE Is serious. Is serious.

CHUCK Oh Loose, you got it all wrong. You got any Italians there?

LUCE I cannot to go back to Italy – they also they keep me in chains. I cannot to leave.

CHUCK Wait a minute ... who's talking about leaving. We just moved in here ...

LUCE [*Stares at him, hating him.*] Here I must always be waiting for you. Is serious!
[*Long pause.*]

CHUCK Okay ... I'll show you serious. You want America – there's America. [*Slowly and deliberately tears a page out of the book.*] You want Germany – [*Tears.*] There's Germany ... You want –

LUCE Listen!

CHUCK Listen to me for a change.

Scene Ten

LUCE Listen to what? To your ugly music? I was thinking you are good musician. I make mistake. Is my mistake, not yours.

CHUCK Shut up.

LUCE This terrible place – you must see –

CHUCK I said shut up.

LUCE Fish and fog. Fish and fog – Halifax!

CHUCK You heard me –

LUCE If I leave –

CHUCK Go! Get out. Go!

LUCE Where?

CHUCK Just go. Just go that's all. [Puts his head in his hands.]

LUCE [Puts her arm around him.] Oh Chuck, I am sorry –

CHUCK Get away.

LUCE I –

CHUCK I'm gonna make it. I'm gonna make it, I promised you that didn't I? If I promised you nothing else – it's getting better. I'm getting more bookings –

LUCE You must to practise.

CHUCK Yeah ... yeah ... [Goes to the piano.] Listen ... what do you think of this? [Begins to play and sing 'The Tennessee Waltz' in an imitative style, stops.] We gotta find my song, that's all ... that's all. [Continues playing.]

Scene Eleven

The farm in Alberta, 1953. DIANA *has gardening gloves, a trowel, and an assortment of seeds. She is making a plan of the flower garden.* PAUL *comes in and looks over her shoulder.*

DIANA [Picking up the seed catalogue.] Will camellias grow d'you think? This catalogue says ...
[PAUL doesn't answer.]

PAUL There's no necessity to stock the ponds this year.

DIANA What?

PAUL Too uncertain.

DIANA [Dismissive.] Paul!

PAUL Let someone else lose their shirt.

DIANA Oh come off it.

PAUL Too chancy. It could be years before we see any return.

DIANA I don't want to listen to this.

PAUL I talked to the accountant today.

DIANA We're going to change the economy of the region. Well, fish farming's the coming –

PAUL We can't afford to take those kinds of risks. Not now.

DIANA You do this every time! Just when we're on the point of making a success of something – bingo! You're not doing another about-turn.

PAUL There's Nigel to think of now.

DIANA What's he got to do with it?

PAUL He's gotta have something better than I did. I had to work to put myself through high school.

DIANA This isn't you talking. What about –

PAUL That's the end of it. I've cancelled out.

DIANA Without consulting me?

PAUL Finished.

DIANA You never cease to amaze me! [*Gathers her things together, furious.*]

PAUL What's this? [*Picks up a package of seeds.*]

DIANA [*Suddenly.*] What if I go ahead on my own?

PAUL You can't. I've cancelled. What are these? [DIANA *snatches the seeds back.*] Canterbury Bells?

DIANA Oh Paul, at least let's talk about this – you can't go through life picking things up and just letting them ... Well, where does it leave me?

PAUL I told you. We can't afford a failure. We can't be a laughing-stock. I don't mind what they say about me, but I don't want them laughing at my son. I know what it's like. They used to laugh at me when I was a kid. It's too risky.

DIANA They laugh because you're so ... so stupid.

PAUL Where did you get these?

DIANA My mother sent them. I was planning to make a real English garden.

PAUL You're not supposed to import seeds, you know that?

DIANA Just a few flowers.

PAUL It's the law. It's the law of this country ...

DIANA Since when were you such a great upholder of the law?

It frightens me Paul, just when I think I know you ...
[PAUL *turns away, about to leave.*] Well, I need flowers.
They're part of my heritage. We've always had flower
gardens. Over here they don't even have fences – hedges
... There's no history. I want my son to have a sense of
his past.

PAUL Only the English would put their history behind a fence.

DIANA That's not what I'm saying. Nigel –

PAUL [*Raising his voice.*] So you think you can show him
history in a package of seeds.

DIANA [*Angry.*] Oh, you don't care ... You don't even know what
it is ... that sense of ... of continuity with ... everything
that's gone before ... You don't have a history.

PAUL What? Do you know when Kiev was founded?

DIANA Kiev!

PAUL Yes. Kiev – that's my history.

DIANA That's ridiculous. You've never even been there. You
know what I'm talking about ... you brought me here
and wiped out my past. Are you going to tell me you've
stopped loving me now?

PAUL What's that got to do with it? God, women! What do you
want from me?

DIANA I'd like to be able to rely on you, that's all –

PAUL What do I have to do to convince you?

DIANA Admit that you're wrong just once.

PAUL Okay, okay, so I shoot for the moon sometimes.

DIANA The moon? Half the solar system as well –

PAUL Okay. Okay, so I admit it.

DIANA What? What do you admit?

PAUL Everything!

DIANA See?

PAUL So I've been a bastard!

DIANA Oh, what's the use?

PAUL Well, you knew what you were in for before you married
me! [DIANA *looks at* PAUL. *Long pause.*] I've led you a
hell of a dance, haven't I? [DIANA *shrugs, choked up.*] I'm
sorry. I'm sorry, Di. I just ... guess I've been selfish.

DIANA [*Stares at him, unbelieving.*] That's the first time I've ever
heard you actually say ...

PAUL I know ...

91

[PAUL *is close to tears. They embrace.*]

DIANA [*Laughs.*] Oh, Paul, you look like a donkey, and I sound like an old fish-wife.

PAUL You are an old fish-wife!

DIANA Not any more! You're not going to stock the ponds!

PAUL You always have to have the last word, don't you?

DIANA Do I?

PAUL Typical WASP. Why'd I marry you?

DIANA Because you're a bohunk donkey, that's why!

Scene Twelve

CHUCK *and* LUCE*'s apartment, Halifax, 1952.* CHUCK *is playing and singing 'Mona Lisa, Mona Lisa How I Love You.'* LUCE *is packing a suitcase.* CHUCK *stops playing and looks at* LUCE.

CHUCK No mi ami.

LUCE Speak English. I cannot stand your terrible Italian.

CHUCK You do not love me, you bitch.

LUCE Love?

CHUCK Love.

LUCE [*Amused.*] I took your name – only for love would I take such a terrible name.

CHUCK You think that?

LUCE Rotten flesh?

CHUCK Basta! Ascoltate! Basta!

LUCE Speak English.

CHUCK I have the right to speak Italian.

LUCE Then speak it well.
[*Pause.*]

CHUCK Why didn't you say you didn't want my name?

LUCE Why didn't you say you intended to live all your life in Halifax?

CHUCK There's nothing wrong with Halifax.

LUCE No? Sure is nothing wrong. Is not even possible to drink wine in a restaurant, is possible smoke opium, but is not possible drink wine – is hypocrite town – no culture.

CHUCK Why didn't you say what you wanted before you came?

LUCE Many things I did not know how to say Chuck. No ...

was not language. Not English, not Italian ... how to
make you understand ... How to make you hear when
you do not know how to listen. [*Pause.*] Not listen to
words but ... [*Reaches down inside herself, then gives up,
shrugs.*] Ach – the whole what you are is ... Canadian.

CHUCK You think you corner the market in sensibility because
you're some high class dago bitch? Mussolini was an
Italian. [LUCE *shrugs.*] I was ashamed, you know that?
When I was in Italy, I always said I was a Maritimer.
Canada may be a desert but at least we don't breed
thugs. Black shirts!

LUCE You breed only bores!

CHUCK What's that supposed to mean?

LUCE It means I am going to Toronto.

CHUCK For the two hundredth time – n ... o ... no.

LUCE [*Quietly.*] It means ... I cannot wait for you any longer
Chuck. I am more than thirty years old. Time is passing
– too much time. I am older than you.

CHUCK You never would have been a singer – you know that.
That's why you came here in the first place, you were a
second-rater and you knew it. That's why you'd never
go off to study when I gave you your chances. That's
why you made out you were going off your head.

LUCE So this time I go. Maybe this time I do go off my head ...
this time I go as far as I can. I find out what is inside me.

CHUCK No ... no. I won't let you.
[CHUCK *empties* LUCE's *suitcase. She picks it up calmly.*]

LUCE I have already accepted to go. You cannot stop me!
[*Pause.*]

CHUCK Okay, so okay. We'll make it Toronto. You win.

LUCE No. No. No. No. I see now –

CHUCK What do you see?

LUCE That you have no ambition. Only dreams. Dreams and
compromises.

CHUCK So you don't compromise eh? You refuse to talk Italian.
You refuse to even acknowledge where you're from and
you take a job as a hostess on an Italian radio show in a
city you say you hate. That's not a compromise?

LUCE It will not be for long. Soon I get into another show ...
maybe television.

CHUCK Television? this time next year it'll be dead. [LUCE

93

shrugs, continues to pack. CHUCK *watches, helpless.*]
Listen, Loose. It's not too late – we could still have a kid
... I'm making good money. The old man's getting old
now – he keeps asking, now that mama's gone. He's got
money put aside – wants to make an investment – he
was talking about maybe opening up a coffee bar. Well,
you could learn to bake. We could hire someone to look
after the kid ...

LUCE I already have a kid. [*Smiles at him.*]

CHUCK Well, what am I? How am I supposed to make you stay?
How long would you be gone for?

LUCE Maybe not for long ... [*Snaps the suitcase shut.*]

Scene Thirteen

Hamilton, 1955. RUTH *and* DAVE *are alone in the kitchen.*

RUTH [*Looking up.*] Oh ... I didn't expect you. [DAVE *stands
looking at* RUTH.] Weren't you going down the Legion?

DAVE There's a meeting on – Remembrance Day committee.

RUTH Oh? I thought you were on it.

DAVE Did I see Jamie on the street?

RUTH He can play on the street.

DAVE He can't.

RUTH They all do. I can't have them under my feet.

DAVE I don't want my kids on the street, okay? What's she
going to think about it? [*Nods toward inner room.*]

RUTH I don't ask her.

DAVE Well remember ... [DAVE *walks into a chair.* RUTH *giggles.*]
Goddammit. Can't you keep things tidy? What does it
take? Do I have to do everything myself?

RUTH It's your mother's chair, not mine. [*Pause.*] I took them
to the doctor's today for their jabs.

DAVE How much did it cost?

RUTH You told me not to take them to the free clinic.

DAVE You coulda waited.

RUTH Did you ask your mother about baby-sitting tonight?
[*Pause.*] She's in there, watching TV.

DAVE We're not going out tonight.

RUTH But you prom ... Oh.

DAVE We can't be going out every night.

RUTH We haven't been out in six months.

DAVE Who's fault is that? Look at you – you should make friends.

RUTH Who with? I can't even have people in ... She ...

DAVE Ssssssssh.

RUTH Well, in Scotland you can just go and knock on anyone's door and they'll go down to the pub with you. You won't even dance now ... In Scotland they're kicking up their heels 'til they're eighty. No one here even picks up a couple of spoons and clacks them. Where are your songs?

DAVE No one wants to sing. Who wants to sing when ...?

RUTH [*Sensing something.*] When what?

DAVE Nothing. [*Pause.*] I quit today.

RUTH Oh Dave!

DAVE [*Mocking.*] Oh Dave!

RUTH But why?

DAVE They were all on my back, that's why. They gave me a week to join their lousy union.

RUTH Who?

DAVE The guys on the floor – the guys I work with, who else? It's a free country, isn't it?

RUTH Oh Dave!

DAVE Is that all you can say?

RUTH But why? Why didn't you just join and keep quiet?

DAVE It's the principle, isn't it? This is a free country, that's what the war was about.

RUTH They're not gonna throw eggs at our door again are they?

DAVE I told you, I quit. They can't call me a scab this time. I didn't come back for people to start pushing me around – pushing socialism down my throat.

RUTH But it's not socialism Dave – it's for the workers.

DAVE I'm a worker aren't I? And I don't want it. I done a good job ... punching in on their lousy clock, shitting myself if I was five minutes late ... sweating to keep their lousy machines running.

RUTH Whose machines?

DAVE The company's.

RUTH But whose side are you on?

DAVE I'm on my side that's what. I got a wife and four kids to
look after –

RUTH [*Quietly, patting her stomach.*] Five.

DAVE I don't have to take orders from no one. I'll do it myself.
I'll tell you this, it's the last time I work for any lousy
steel company.

RUTH Did you try at Dofasco?

DAVE You gotta have an in.
[*Pause.*]

RUTH I could get a job if your mum'd ... I worked before ... in
the fish market.

DAVE No wife of mine works.

RUTH If we got a typewriter I could learn to type. If we could
afford –

DAVE I done it right, didn't I? I went over there, I fought for
this country – I love this country, right? I come back – I
play by the rules.
[*Pause.*]

DAVE How come other guys got all the luck? Guys who
weren't even over there?

RUTH It's just luck that's all.
[RUTH *holds out her hand to him. He knocks it away and
swipes her drink off the table.*]

Scene Fourteen

*Staging of this scene is dependent on costume changes.
Ideally, all characters should be in position at the
opening of the scene and each is spotlit as he or she
speaks. However, where production logistics do not allow
for this, characters should step into positions whenever
appropriate.*

New Year's Eve, 1957. LUCE *is broadcasting in Toronto.*
RUTH *is sitting at the kitchen table, a blank sheet of paper
in front of her, a drink to hand, staring straight ahead.*
CHUCK *is playing in a bar, no audience.* DAVE *is in the*

Legion, wearing his Legion tie, sitting near the Union Jack. PAUL *is at his father's farm in Saskatchewan, shovelling snow.* DIANA *is clearing snow in their drive in Alberta.*

LUCE Felice anno nuovo, auguri a tutti voi acoltatori della radio Italo-Toronto. Happy New Year! L'ultimo disco del'anno cinquanta sette sarà ... si, lo so, han' indovinato ... 'Che sera, sera'. [*Puts the record on, sound fades.*]

RUTH December thirty-first, 1957. Dear Mum and Dad and everybody. Well, it's the end of another year, and I've a few minutes before I get on with Dave's tea. I wanted to write – you'll be wondering why I haven't written – well to tell you the truth, the sixth one's on the way – Dave's real pleased, he loves children. I'm sending a picture of us all, that's me in the back. As you'll see, young Jamie's just like his dad, a regular film star, and Rita's a tomboy like I used to be, they call her Cissy here for short. The Queen came to Toronto last week. I took all the kids up on the train to see her, but we stood in the wrong place. You'll be pleased to hear that, Dad, I know what you think of all that English stuff. Everyone's giving me lots of presents for the baby, they've got lots of money here in Canada. Well, I've got to go now, I've got him a steak bigger than his plate, so love to Mary and Angus and the kids and everyone. [*Takes a drink.*] Tell Angus to hurry up and come up on the races so he can send me a ticket to come home. I miss you ... no. [*Drinks.*] Love from Ruthie.

CHUCK Right folks, listen to this one. Don Messer, you better watch out for me. [*Plays 'My Old Canadian Home' for a few bars, stops.*] Okay, you guys, so where are you? It's New Year's Eve, there should be someone in here celebrating!

DAVE It's never been the same since the war, eh? [*Drinks beer.*] People aren't the same these days, no values, the spirit's gone out of them. Women – they're all over the place. They're all getting like the Canadian whores they sent over in the war – had their skirts up 'round their necks before they were even off the boat. That's why I married a different kind of girl. Next year I'll bring her down here ... yeah. Happy New Year! [*Drinks.*] If I'd'a let Verna marry me instead'a her marrying Tom ... sitting around all day – air traffic control – what's he know about airplanes? I was shaking hands with Buzz Beurling when Mom was still washing behind his ears. Yeah, take it easy, Buzz old buddy – remember this one could be the last. [*Drinks.*] That's all people want today. Forget about the war, forget about your old mother, leave that to somebody else, forget your responsibilities. Just have the one kid and forget to send him to his first communion, or ask his uncle to be godfather. Just think about holidays in Florida under some goddamn Yankee orange tree where they never even seen a Spitfire. Let someone else stay home and look after your mother's basement when it floods. Wipe out the past. No, that's not what we fought for. They wanna flush all the old standards down the drain. I didn't go over there so's Tom could have a sailboat and a new car every year, and thumb his nose at me. [*Pauses.*] That was the best goddamn time of my life, and I didn't even know it. [CHUCK *sings 'My Old Canadian Home.' Lights up on* PAUL.]

PAUL Snow. Six days of the stuff – ugh. Can't leave him alone for many more winters. He'll break his neck. Put him in a home ... he'll die ... must talk to her about it. How? He doesn't even think of her as a person ... Anglicki ... Well, I'm not gonna keep coming out to Saskatchewan every New Year's. Deserves to break his neck. Jesus, how come with all their high-flown technology they can't look after the old folks ... Politicians! Someone should come up with a way of straightening out their priorities. Just needs a bit of vision. Someone with overall vision. Energy. Where's it gone? Energy to start over?

DIANA Snow to see the new year in. And for the next four months ... endless ... [*Stares out into the distance.*] It was the flatness that terrified me. It doesn't bother me now. Funny ... I can think about all that – couldn't then – numb. I remember thinking if I talked about it – if I even thought about it – I wouldn't be able to go on. If he'd

only let me have a radio – that weekly paper! I couldn't
laugh about it. My jaws were frozen. Had to shut it all
out ... There are times – there were times, when I'd look
at the sky and wonder if it would be the same sky that
they were seeing back home, or was it some other
planet? It was so flat ... and so cold in winter – the first
year was the worst. The way you could hear the wolves
and coyotes. I never told him ... I thought I was on the
edge of the world – the flatness under the snow. Aqui
nada. That's what they said the word 'Canada' came
from. When the Spaniards made a map of North
America they wrote it over the top. Where we are now –
aqui nada. Nothing here. The silence ... Then when I
went back home I couldn't sleep for the traffic noises ...
and we didn't even live near a main road. I was – funny
how ashamed I still am of those old feelings – lonely.
[*Shivers, catches her arms around herself.*] But his is my
country now ... I belong here. Paul ... [*Looks around,
suddenly scared.*] Paul, don't stay away.

PAUL [*Still clearing snow in Saskatchewan.*] Couple of hours
and it'll be covered over again. Just keep shovelling. He
says you gotta learn to live with it – adapt – it all takes
time – yeah – generations. But my time isn't that long.
Someone's gotta make the changes. Something's gotta
be done. I built up a good business – I got a decent kid, I
love my wife – what more is there? I'm gonna write that
book now! [*Pauses.*] I'm nearly forty years old. Anyone
can do anything. Di ... [*Pulls his arms around himself.*]
Diana ... [*Shivers.*]
[*Blackout. Lights up and fade on Union Jack as maple leaf
flag is brought into prominence.*]

Scene Fifteen

Montreal, 1966. CHUCK *and* LUCE *have just met on St. Catherine Street.*

CHUCK I can't get over it.

LUCE On St. Catherine Street, just like that.

CHUCK So. Howdeedoodi.

LUCE What?

CHUCK How's it going? You're looking great.

LUCE Oh, not bad. Yourself?

CHUCK [*Grunts twice.*] So. What are you doing in Montreal?

LUCE Learning French, among other things.

CHUCK French?

LUCE Sure.

CHUCK Italian isn't good enough for you?

LUCE Not in this business. Especially not with Expo opening up next year.

CHUCK So. How is business?

LUCE Oh. Pretty good, you know.

CHUCK I saw you in a commercial. Dog food or something.

LUCE Mayonnaise.

CHUCK That's it.

LUCE It's going very well actually. I just cut a record.

CHUCK You did?

LUCE Just a small one.

CHUCK A forty-five?

LUCE Mainly I do voice-overs in commercials. I've started to compose my own melodies. Just for the commercials. [*Pause.*] It's been a long time. It's good to see you, Chuck.

CHUCK Likewise.

LUCE So. What are you doing so far from Halifax?

CHUCK Vacation. You know ... staking out the territory. We thought we might move out here ... but we'll probably head for Ontario. That's where the work is, right?

LUCE We?

CHUCK Oh ... oh, I got married. Didn't you know?

LUCE Who is she? The lucky lady?

CHUCK You remember Rosemary? [LUCE *shakes her head.*] She used to help my dad out. He's really expanded now, three stores ... going great guns.

LUCE I don't remember her.

CHUCK Yes you do. She always did the evening shift. Anyway, it's her.

LUCE Are you happy?

CHUCK Sure are. Hey, you should meet her – she'd like that. She's back at the motel. First vacation we've taken in five years. With the kids and all.

LUCE Ah.

CHUCK Two boys.

LUCE Congratulations. I seem to be repeating myself.

CHUCK I got a pretty good act together. Mostly Italian numbers – really suits my style. Hey ... are you going to be around for a while? I'm trying to arrange a couple of bookings at a place in Sherbrooke while we're here.

LUCE No ... no. I have to get back. We start rehearsals on Monday.

CHUCK What for?

LUCE Just a little show. One of those back street cabaret places, you know. Bit of dancing, bit of singing.

CHUCK Dancing? Aren't you a bit old for that? I mean ...

LUCE Oh, I keep in shape.

CHUCK Yeah.

LUCE It's just a group of friends. We got together and wrote this thing. It'll probably bomb.

CHUCK No way. I'm probably going to be in Toronto – maybe I'll catch it. Got a couple of people to see – Holiday Inn – you know it?

LUCE Oh, is Gary Richter still the manager?

CHUCK I don't remember the guy's name ...

LUCE Maybe I can do something for you. Here. [*Gives him her card.*] Why don't you give me a call when you get into town.

CHUCK Yeah. Yeah, sure I will. So ... I should be getting along

now. Can't keep the little lady waiting. Good meeting
you Loose. Let's keep in touch now we found each
other, eh?

LUCE Yeah. Yeah. Let's do that. [*They embrace.*] Au revoir,
Chuck.

CHUCK Ci vediamo. [*Chucks her under the chin and leaves.*]

Scene Sixteen

RUTH *and* DAVE's *kitchen, Hamilton, 1967.* RUTH *is locked
out, slightly tipsy, yelling at the back door.*

RUTH [*Sings. Tune: 'Scots Wha Hae.'*]
   Wha will be a traitor knave,
   wha can fill a coward's grave;
   wha sae base a be a slave?
   Traitor, coward turn and flee ...
Okay, so the kids are asleep. I can shout if I like ... I don't
care if she hears – can ye hear me mother? You'd better
let me in, Dave. No ... you wouldn't dare do anything.
[*Expectant pause. Sings. Tune: 'Bluebells of Scotland.'*]
   Oh it's where tell me where has my bonnie laddie
gone?
   He's gone to bonnie Scotland where the sweet
bluebells grow ...
I had a wee dance tonight, Dave – while you were
watching your hockey ... Well, aren't you surprised? ...
Come on out and hit me. They were singing Scottish
songs ... They asked us to come back next Friday – me
and Molly McLaren. We danced ... on the tables. We did
so! Aye. [*Giggles.*] They don't really like us here, me and
Molly. They don't like us, 'cos we're not Canadians. And
I'll tell you something. [*Giggles.*] We don't like them
either. [*Sticks out her tongue childishly.*]
[DAVE *comes to the door, pulls* RUTH *roughly into the
room, and shoves her into a chair.*]

DAVE I'm going back up to bed. And don't you dare come near
those stairs!

Scene Seventeen

La Gondola Restaurant, Niagara Falls, 1970. CHUCK *plays 'I Never Promised You a Rose Garden' in an Italian version. His style is exaggeratedly Mediterranean, smooth.* DIANA, PAUL, RUTH *and* DAVE *are eating in silence at a table illuminated by a single candle.* LUCE *sits nearby, smartly dressed and coiffed, alone at a table.*

PAUL So ... what would you recommend we do with our time here?

DAVE How long do you have?

PAUL A few days. We're going to the ballet on Tuesday night – in Toronto.

DAVE If you'd'a timed it better you coulda taken in a home game.

DIANA Oh yes? You have a rather good football team here don't you?

DAVE Only the best in the country. She prefers soccer. [*Meaning* RUTH.]

RUTH You like it too. Dundee's doing good this year – I still listen to the Scottish League results on Saturdays, do you? They can't pronounce the names.

DIANA I hear it was quite something when they won the World Cup.

RUTH Aye – that was England.

DIANA I was never very big on sports. Paul is.

PAUL Sure am. I like to get out there and curl. [*To* DAVE.] How about you?

DAVE Curl up in bed!

DIANA Tell them about the bowling league. He's been King Pin for three years in a row.

PAUL What we need is a few more hours to the day.

DIANA It's been an enormously ... full life.

DAVE Full?

DIANA [*Signalling* PAUL *to help her out.*] I mean ... it still is.

PAUL You're dead right. We hardly see each other. [*To* RUTH.]

103

You know this is the longest time I've spent alone with
my wife since ... for about twenty years.

RUTH But don't you live together?

PAUL Sure. But you try living with someone who heads up
just about every goddamned committee that's going!
And if there isn't one going she'll start it up.

DIANA You speak for yourself. He's so involved in politics he
hardly manages to get time for supper more than twice
a week. It's a good job he has an efficient manager.

PAUL And an efficient wife! [*Laughs.*]

DIANA We both have to be.

[PAUL *and* DIANA *smile at each other.* DAVE *looks
disgusted.*]

PAUL Come on Ruth, what about a dance?

RUTH [*Looks at* DAVE.] Oh ... maybe when there's a few more
people ...

PAUL I'm a bit rusty but I'm not that bad.

RUTH I didn't mean that!

PAUL Come on then.

[PAUL *gets up and pulls* RUTH's *chair back. They dance.*
DAVE *and* DIANA *are alone at the table.*]

RUTH Are you really in politics?

PAUL I do what I can.

RUTH Oh, I thought maybe I was talking to an MP or
something.

PAUL Strictly a policy man.

[*Pause.*]

RUTH You're a nice dancer.

PAUL I have two left feet.

RUTH Do you do it often? Dance, I mean.

PAUL Not if I can avoid it.

RUTH You're as bad as Dave! What's she on? The committees.
You said –

PAUL Oh ... the library board ... civil liberties, things like that.
I'll never persuade her to give them up – says she's the
only one who's ever read anything.

RUTH She was always a bit hoity toity – oh, I shouldn't say
that. Would you like to come to our house? I mean ...
maybe tomorrow? You could come for a drink – Dave
can come and get you.

PAUL We rented a car.

RUTH Then you'll come?

PAUL I guess so. We'd like that, yes.

RUTH I'd ask you to supper, only ...

PAUL We wouldn't expect you to do anything like that.

RUTH About eight o'clock?

PAUL I'll have to confirm with the boss!

RUTH Oh, she'll say yes

[*Pause. PAUL laughs and pulls RUTH a little closer. They do a fancy step.*]

DAVE So ... who's looking after your place then? The manager?

DIANA Yes. It's the first time we've left him – I hope it'll be all right. He's quite young – barely out of agricultural school – not much older than Nigel – our son.

[*Silence, then DAVE and DIANA together.*]

DIANA I was thinking –

DAVE You ever thought –

DIANA I'm sorry.

DAVE Go ahead.

DIANA No, it wasn't important.

[*Silence.*]

DAVE I was gonna say ... whether you've ever thought how it would've been if there hadn't been a war? Well, you wouldn't be over here for a start.

DIANA God no. I'd've been married to some stuffy stockbroker probably.

DAVE You don't think you'd'a been better off?

DIANA No.

DAVE I don't know. How come you Brits always have to tell us what to do?

DIANA Oh c'mon. You know that's not true. [*Pause.*] Well, I can't say I haven't had an exciting life. I never knew what Paul was going to throw at me next.

DAVE [*With renewed interest.*] He doesn't look the type.

DIANA I'm speaking metaphorically.

DAVE Oh. [*Silence.*] Is he always that way?

DIANA What way?

DAVE With women?

[*PAUL and RUTH glance across at DAVE and return to the area of the table.*]

PAUL Loosen up the old limbs.

RUTH Let's dance Dave.

DAVE You shoulda married Fred Astaire. [*Makes no effort to rise.*]

RUTH Ach!

PAUL I've got an idea. What do you think of this? [*Whispers to* RUTH.]

RUTH Oh yes!

[PAUL *goes over to* CHUCK. DIANA *turns and watches, curious.*]

DIANA He's such a silly.

[RUTH *sits at the table and starts to peel the label off the wine bottle.*]

DAVE What are you doing?

RUTH [*Whispering.*] I have to remember the name.

DAVE What for?

RUTH They're coming for a drink on Sunday night.

DAVE What?

RUTH Sssh!

[DAVE *grabs the label and puts it back on the bottle.* DIANA *catches this, turns and smiles.* PAUL *returns to the table.*]

DIANA Let's dance Paul.

PAUL No, not yet. Wait a minute.

RUTH [*To* PAUL.] Dance with me.

PAUL We'll sit this one out. [*To* DIANA] I want you to listen – [CHUCK *switches tunes and begins to sing and play 'Diana.'*] Well?

DIANA Nice.

DAVE Your song eh? [DIANA *nods.*] They should get Ruthie up there.

RUTH Me?

DAVE [*Not being sarcastic.*] Sure.

DIANA Do you sing, Ruthie?

RUTH No.

PAUL I'll bet you do.

DAVE You should hear her. She should be with that White Heather show, you know that? [*To* DIANA.] You sing those songs too?

DIANA Oh no. I run the choir – we managed a full-scale

'Messiah' last year. We had guest soloists from Calgary.
[CHUCK *stops playing and begins to speak with an
assumed Italian accent.*]

CHUCK Good evening ladies and gentlemen and welcome to La
Gondola, the ship of dreams, afloat in the honeymoon
capital of the world. As usual, a special hello to all of
you newlyweds out there. Some of your faces I
recognize from last year, and even before that – and you
know what – you still look like you're in love! Well, I got
bad news for you, folks – I'm abandoning ship. Yes, last
week I signed a contract with a famous hotel chain that
shall be nameless. It is enough to say that from the first
of next month I'll be appearing nightly in the Blue Room
at a certain hotel in Toronto. [*Applause.*] I have invited
the lady who is responsible for the Holiday Inn's good
fortune – whoops! – to be here with me for my last
night. Just back from New York, let me present the very
lovely Luce Marini. [*Pronounces her name correctly.
Applause.*] Luce! [*Drinks to her, raises glass to the
audience.*] Since this is my last night at La Gondola, I
offer a drink on the house to everyone. [*Applause. He
begins to play and sing 'Lonely is the Man Without Love'
in Italian.*] 'Quando m'inamoro ...'

DAVE Love ... why don't they sing about something else?

RUTH Like what?

DAVE Work. [*To* PAUL.] Well why not? ... [*Nods at* CHUCK.]
That's woman's stuff eh?

DIANA She's quite nice looking. I've seen her in commercials.

RUTH He's good looking too. We'll have to watch out for his
show. D'you think I could ask them for their autograph?
Janet'd like it. Maybe they'd sign this. [*Meaning the
menu.*]

DAVE That goes with the furniture. [RUTH *gets up.*] Hey ...
come back here ...
[RUTH *takes the menu over the* CHUCK.]

DIANA She can't be as young as she looks.

PAUL That's show biz eh? Look at Mae West.

DAVE Who wants to?

CHUCK What's your name?

RUTH [*Glancing at* DAVE.] Janet.

CHUCK [*Signs with a flourish.*] Ciao Janet.

[RUTH *goes to* LUCE.]

LUCE No, I don't give autographs.

RUTH Oh … I'm sorry. [*Pause.*] We're celebrating you see. It's their anniversary. We knew each other in the war.

LUCE Oh? So did we … [*Glances at* CHUCK.]

RUTH Everything … changes doesn't it? [RUTH *smiles shyly.* LUCE *relents and signs.*] I'm sorry to bother you … thank you.

[RUTH *goes back to the table.* LUCE *picks up her jacket.* CHUCK *puts out his hand to stop her.*]

CHUCK Don't go.

LUCE [*Smiles.*] Don't worry – I'll wait.

CHUCK One more set and we can leave.

[CHUCK *continues to play.* LUCE *sits back, smiling.*]

PAUL [*To* DAVE.] So … what do you think of Mr. Trudeau?

RUTH [*Warning.*] Dave!

DIANA Paul headed up our local campaign committee at the last election. We got to know Eugene Whelan personally, didn't we sweetie? [*Hiccoughs.*] Oh … I think I'm getting a bit tipsy.

RUTH They're very nice. They're Italian. I don't think he's the owner.

DAVE War measures … yeah! We need more of that strong-arm stuff.

PAUL So you've never been back to Scotland Ruthie?

RUTH If I'd a gone to Scotland … I was afraid I … I just might not've come back.

DAVE Eh? You hear that? [*Laughs at the absurdity of the idea.*]

RUTH The kids want me to leave him. They have it all worked out. They're talking about renting a wee flat for me and Janet and Craigie … the others don't need me now. [*Pause.*] Rita says it's for the best. I wonder if he's going to play again? Maybe he knows some of the old songs. [*Long silence.* CHUCK *begins to play 'La Novia.'*]

DIANA [*Brightly.*] Talking of going home, the last time I was in the old country they seemed to think I was some kind of hillbilly.

RUTH My dad died. I don't think of him as dead.

DIANA Oh, I'm sorry! Well, this is our home now isn't it. It's certainly mine. It's not that I've given up – that is – I'll always be English, but I'm Canadian as well. This is where I belong. Isn't that right?

RUTH I'm a grandmother now. Rita got married right out of university. She graduated.

DIANA You must be very proud.

RUTH She married a Scotsman. His family came over with Bonnie Prince Charlie – well, not with him, bu –

DIANA I'm rather glad Nigel's not married yet – it would make us feel so old. He still hangs around the yard. Long hair – all he reads is left-wing propaganda. If you talked to him you'd think he was illiterate. Young people today! He's a strange boy – spends all his spare time learning Ukrainian. What earthly use is that going to be to him? [DAVE *stands up, as if to leave.*]

PAUL Where are you going?

DAVE What's that to you?

RUTH Sit down.

DAVE And you ... [*Gestures at* RUTH, *picks up a glass.*]

DIANA How many children do you have?

RUTH Six.

DIANA Six. Oh, do sit down, Dave. [DAVE *smashes the glass.* PAUL *goes around the table to stop him.* DAVE *pushes him roughly.* DIANA *rushes over to* PAUL. DAVE *looks around, stops, brings his fist down on the table.*]

DAVE Okay, you're gonna listen to me for a change. You're gonna listen to me. There's nothing wrong with the way I am – I can't help it if I'm not a goddamned Scotsman –

RUTH I never wanted you to –

DAVE There's nothing wrong with this country either. This country is the greatest in the world.

PAUL Here here.

DIANA No one's arguing with you Dave. [LUCE *joins* CHUCK *at the piano.*]

DAVE I'm sick of hearing you run it down. It's the best goddamned country in ... You should be grateful to be here. All of you ... [*Shouts.*] All of you. I fought for Canada. It's the greatest goddamned country in the world, so what's the matter with you all? You name one that's better. Scotland? Don't make me laugh. England? It's a joke.

RUTH [*Gets up, clutching her purse, which obviously contains a bottle.*] Excuse me.

DAVE And you don't have to go out there to take a drink. You can have one right here. We're gonna drink to our kids, and to Canada. [*Pours* RUTH *a drink.*] Where are those free drinks?

DIANA [*Raising her glass.*] To us, to all of us, and to Canada.

DAVE Where's the music? What's happened to the goddamned music? [LUCE *whispers to* CHUCK. *He plays the opening of 'Somewhere Over the Rainbow.'* LUCE *begins to sing.*] She's been the best wife a man could have and I won't let any of you say any different.

[DAVE *stares at* RUTH, *then goes over to her slowly and kisses her hand.*]

RUTH Oh Dave.

[RUTH *and* DAVE *dance, holding each other closely.* LUCE *and* CHUCK *sing in duet.* DIANA *and* PAUL *raise their glasses to each other, put them down, and dance.*]

END

Words to Italian Songs

'Rose Garden' [*chorus only,* CHUCK's *version.*]
Mi dispiace
Non ti prometto belle rose
Ore di sole
E giornate quando piove.
C'è un momento quando dai
E oltre non fa mai
Lo so-o-o-o-o
Mi dispiace ...

'La Novia' [*The Wedding.*]
Bianch'e splendente
E la novia.
Mentre nascosta
Tra la folla
Dietr'una lacrima
Indecisa
Vedo morir le mie' illusioni
Là sull' altar
Lei sta piangendo.
Tutti dirano
Che di gioia,
Mentre il suo cuor'
Sta gridando.
Ave Maria.

'Lonely Is the Man Without Love' [CHUCK's *version.*]
Quando m'inamoro
Sarà un tesoro
Quando trovo quella per me.
Se quel'giorno viene
P'are che non viene
Solo son'un uomo senza amor'.

DIVING

Notes

Diving was first produced by the New Play Centre, Vancouver, March 1983 with Wendy Goroing as Viveca and direction by Larry Lillo.

Diving

The stage is completely bare.
   VIVECA enters. She is thin, almost scrawny. She wears
a pair of clogs. She carries a bag. She looks around,
scared. Kicks off her clogs. Stops, thinks – has she
forgotten something? She remembers. She takes a small
box from between her breasts, careful not to uncover
herself. She opens the box and takes earplugs out. Inserts
plugs in ears. She puts the box down carefully next to the
clogs which she lines up with precision. She shivers.
   A male voice is heard off stage.

MALE VOICE Dive Viveca.
   [VIVECA looks up to where the male voice comes from.
   She takes the earplugs out gingerly. Listens. The voice is
   silent. She puts one earplug back. She shades her eyes
   and looks out over the audience. She seems to be looking
   over a vast, deep body of water. She smiles nervously.
   She takes off her towel. She is wearing an absurd
   swimsuit decorated with maple leaves. She folds the
   towel very carefully, trying to make the edges perfect. She
   places it next to the shoes, the box and the bag She
   remembers her nose clamp which she has left in a locker
   offstage and puts her foot into one of her clogs, meaning
   to go and get it.]
MALE VOICE Viveca!
   [She hastily withdraws her foot. She walks over to the
   stairway which leads up to the diving platform. (The
   structure is imaginary.) She puts her hands on the rails
   and takes one step up. She smiles upward, waiting for
   approval from the voice which does not come. She looks
   fearfully over the pool. She takes a tentative step, pulling
   herself up with her arms. She practises the diving
   position, very nervous.]
VIVECA I've been watching eagles. They don't close their eyes
   when they dive. They transfer the salmon from their
   beak to their claws. [A long silence, as though she has
   forgotten herself.] My mother says that swimming

makes you bulge in all the wrong places. [*Feels her forearms, covers her breasts.*] She wants me to be a dog trainer. She says there's a future in breeding. She has three English sheepdogs. [*A pause. She goes up one step.*] I prefer eagles. She used to take the dogs down to the beach and throw sticks in the water. Retrieve! They never got their feet wet. I'd jump in and paddle out and bring the sticks back. In my hand – not in my mouth, in my hand. [*Shows how, spluttering, half drowning.*] No one told me it was easier in bare feet. Some things you learn by experience. An eagle never has to learn. But an eagle doesn't wear shoes in the first place. [*Laughs.*] Dogs she'd say, dogs are sensible. [*She looks up to see if anyone will notice if she dashes down the steps. Takes a tentative step down.*]

MALE VOICE Dive Viveca! [*She goes back to where she was on the steps. Goes a few steps higher.*]

VIVECA I moved out of her house and I rented an upstairs apartment. No animals allowed it said. It was written up there on the entrance. By the mail slots. 'Sorry no pets.' That meant no snakes, no lizards, no small furry creatures. Not even a cricket in a cage. [*Pause.*] It was a lovely apartment. Just one room, but on the 15th floor – and a balcony. And there was a supermarket down below, and a carpark and all these small cars like cockroaches coming and going, but what I could see most was the sky. [*She looks out into the distance over the heads of the audience.*] I used to stand on the balcony. [*She raises her arms.*] Once they called the fire truck and they shouted at me through a megaphone, and they brought my mother and she let herself in with the spare key. Apparently there's a rule about standing on your balcony ... [*She goes up two more steps, very proud. Looks around.*] My mother gave me a dog for my birthday. It was a very small dog, she said no one would notice it. It used to whine, and when the caretaker asked about the noise I told him it was me. He told me I should see someone. He used to come to my door and listen and I'd watch him listening through the peephole – the pink top of his head, or a pink chin or his ring

116

finger with no ring. When I went down the hallway I used to whine outside his door. [*She moves up a couple of steps.*] Then I moved to the 'Y.' I left the dog behind. It didn't have a name. I called it dog. Dog come here, Dog fetch, Dog jump. Over the balcony, down to the parking lot. [*She laughs.*] Dive dog!

MALE VOICE Dive Viveca! [*She looks up fearfully.*]

VIVECA But he didn't. Dogs don't.

MALE VOICE Dive! [*She runs up three more steps.*]

VIVECA They have a pool at the 'Y.' No pets allowed. Dog followed me. He had to stay outside. He sat by the steps till I came out, and then he walked as far as the dry-cleaning shop and sat outside till I finished work. That's how stupid dogs are. Fetch dog. Sit dog. Laugh dog. Obey! Eagles don't.

MALE VOICE Dive! [*She walks up another step petulantly.*]

VIVECA No one ever tells me what to do.

MALE VOICE Dive Viveca.

VIVECA Mrs. Martin at the shop says I'm one of those born lucky people who just don't need to be told anything. So why does she keep telling me? [*Long pause. She stares out over the pool, shivers suddenly, backs down a step. The* MALE VOICE *clears its throat and* VIVECA *races up several steps.*] It's high up here. [*Looks up at platform.*] But not too high. [*Pause.*] Salmon. Salmon leap high up falls. I know, I've seen them. And in October they flap in the shallows and leap up and get caught in low branches, and there they stay, skeletons with their eyes pecked out. But before – before, the water's so thick with swimmers that you could walk on it, and banks lined with black crows, waiting. And fishermen at the falls with lures. And then the salmon are born again and theres no more river to swim up so they turn around and swim down and dive down the falls. Isn't that right? It's called a life cycle.

MALE VOICE Dive Viveca. [*She makes up her mind. Walks up the last steps, reaches the platform, walks along the length of it, balancing. Goes to the edge and looks down. Draws her breath. Retreats almost losing her balance. Stretches her body. Stretches her arms. Stands on tiptoe. Breathes deer*

VIVECA Like an arc, like a bridge, like a hammock with the wind under it. [*Arches her body. Playfully.*] Dive dog.

MALE VOICE [*Commanding.*] Viveca!

VIVECA Dog!

MALE VOICE Viveca! [*VIVECA laughs.*] Dive! [*VIVECA barks and* MALE VOICE *continues in a warning manner.*] Viveca. [*She whimpers.*] Dive!

VIVECA [*She gets ready, stands in perfect position, poised.*] Dog, dog, where are you?

MALE VOICE Now!

VIVECA Yes?

MALE VOICE Yes.

VIVECA Yes.

MALE VOICE Yes!

VIVECA Now! [*She dives, lights snap off. Blackout. A spot roams around the stage looking for her and finds the skeleton of a salmon dangling at the level where* VIVECA's *head was. A disembodied male soprano voice sings 'Oh For the Wings of a Dove.' The lights and music fade to black and then the lights come up full.* VIVECA *enters briskly, no longer wearing leaves. She wears a jaunty maple-leaf patterned swimsuit and carries the towel over her shoulder. She hums a pop tune as she prepares to enter the water while putting in her earplugs and kicking off her clogs. She takes a tape recorder from her bag, switches it on and adjusts her nose clamp while she listens. The voice on the tape is the same* MALE VOICE *but the note of command has gone.*]

MALE VOICE Lesson two. [*Snatch of pop music.*] Now that you have mastered the preliminary exercise, stand waist deep in the water. Extend the arms above the head and bend forward at the waist; bend the knees slightly and focus your eyes on the bottom of the pool. [*VIVECA tries but is confused. She bends, rewinds the tape. The* MALE VOICE *is reduced to gibberish. It starts again and* VIVECA *follows the instructions as the lights go down. Half light lingers on her briefly as she stands, staring at bottom of the pool.*]

FADE

END

ISLANDS

Notes

Islands was first produced by the New Play Centre, Vancouver, at the Waterfront Theatre in February and March, 1983, with the following cast:

ALLI *Anna Hagan*
MURIEL *Patricia Ludwick*
ROSE *Doris Chilcott*
DIRECTOR *Kate Weiss*

Characters:
MURIEL *Mid thirties*
ROSE *Muriel's mother*
ALLI *Mid to late forties*

Author's note: *Islands* is a companion piece to *Alli Alli Oh* available from the Playwrights Union of Canada). If *Islands* is not performed in conjunction with *Alli Alli Oh*, the following should be omitted:
ALLI There was no hammock in the hospital. No lawn. Only a concrete parking lot.

The Setting:
A house on an island off the west coast of Canada. The house is fairly roughly furnished, with unfinished insulation. The furniture is of the rough-hewn, farmhouse variety. There is a wood stove – a two-burner electric stove sits on top. Part of the porch is visible on the set, separated by a screen door. There should be a door to the bedroom.

The stage is lit by a bare electric bulb. Other props include a record player, TV, and radio. A small neatly made-up bed stands to one side of the room.

Islands

MURIEL *is alone on the stage, working on a partially constructed desk / drawing board, which she is assembling. Soft music from the record player. She moves to the record player and changes the record. She is relaxed, leisurely. Goes back to her work.* ROSE *enters carrying a large bunch of flowers.*

ROSE   I hope you don't mind. I thought I'd brighten the place a bit.

MURIEL   [*Without looking up.*] There's a vase somewhere. [*During the following exchanges* ROSE *distributes the flowers among likely looking containers.*]

ROSE   What are you doing?

MURIEL   Drawing board.

ROSE   [*Persists.*] What for?

MURIEL   [*Absorbed.*] I can't work properly sitting down. [*Nods to the blueprints on the table.*]

ROSE   Did you wonder where I was?

MURIEL   [*Dutifully.*] Where were you?

ROSE   Down at the beach. Dug some more clams for a chowder.

MURIEL   You'd better get the grit out of them this time.

ROSE   Mind if I turn this thing off? [*Without waiting for a reply,* ROSE *turns the record player off.*] The tide was out. Way out. I think I prefer it that way. I don't feel so crowded.

MURIEL   [*Concentrating on her work.*] You can use the boat if you like. I'll put it on the truck and take it down to the ramp.

ROSE   Me? In that? [*Laughs.*] Come on.

MURIEL   It probably leaks anyway. Been out in the yard all winter. Needs a coat of paint.

ROSE   I could do that for you.

MURIEL   Guess you could.

ROSE   You're working too hard. [*No response.*] Why don't you relax a bit? [ROSE *goes over to the table and looks at the blueprints, shifting them.*]

121

MURIEL No ... no ... don't touch them. [ROSE *takes no notice.*]
Mother!

ROSE You can't build a house. [MURIEL *continues to work.*] Not
on your own.

MURIEL I'll get help. If I need it.

ROSE Your grandfather built our house. It nearly killed him.
Look at your hands. [*Pause.*] I'm not against hard work.
I've worked hard all my life. [*Points at the blueprint.*]
That's man's work. [*Long pause.* MURIEL *works.*]

MURIEL I hope you weren't bored today.

ROSE No, no, I wasn't bored. [*Pause.*] What time did you say
the ferry got in?

MURIEL I already told you.

ROSE He must have caught the late one. He'll have the sense
to call. [MURIEL *works.* ROSE *fusses with the flowers.*] You
won't be working when he's here, will you? He won't
want to see you heaving planks. He'll feel he has to give
you a hand.

MURIEL I could use some help.

ROSE He's not well. [MURIEL *gives* ROSE *a sidelong glance.*] He's
gonna be crazy about the beaches. I'd no idea it was this
pretty. We tried to read up on it in the library. You never
described it in your letters.

MURIEL I never wrote.

ROSE Well – Christmas cards. [*Pause.*] I keep going 'round
trying to see everything with his eyes. [MURIEL *works.*]
Muriel – I didn't want to spring it on you this way. I
know you're going to like him.

MURIEL Just as long as he doesn't mind getting his boots
muddy.

ROSE Oh, he's used to farm people. He was in the bank for
thirty-five years. He said they'd have folded up without
the farmers.

MURIEL Sure, they milked every goddamn farmer for miles
around.

ROSE He took an early retirement. On account of his asthma.
[MURIEL *laughs.*] Your brother says I'm doing the right
thing. And you know Ronnie – he's not easy to please.
[ROSE *finishes the flower arrangement, stands back to
admire it.*]

122

MURIEL Looks like a funeral parlour. Don't they bring on asthma?

ROSE [*Laughs.*] No – that's hay fever. He doesn't sneeze, he sniffs. He always has a flower in his buttonhole.

MURIEL [*Points out a flower.*] That's a protected species.

ROSE I only took one or two. They're so pretty. They don't grow in Alberta, do they? I've never seen them.

MURIEL If they did they'd have been wiped out years ago. [ROSE *looks for something to do.*] Why don't you pour yourself a drink?

ROSE You know I don't drink. [*Pause.*] Well just the occasional glass of wine. He knows about wines. When we went to Toronto we had champagne and orange juice for breakfast.

MURIEL To Toronto eh? Wowee!

ROSE Yes. To visit his married daughter.

MURIEL Champagne. And orange juice. And [*derisively*] Chuck.

ROSE Yes. [*Laughs.*] You know we had two bottles of champagne. One was Canadian and one was French, and I bet him he couldn't tell the difference. I tied his necktie 'round his eyes and poured out two glasses of Canadian just to trick him ... then he had to guess which was which.

MURIEL Did he?

ROSE He spat them both out!

MURIEL A man after my own heart!

ROSE He doesn't drink hard liquor. Like your father. He never drank.

MURIEL He used to suck a lot of peppermints.

ROSE What do you know?

MURIEL [*Leaving her work for a moment.*] Remember when he used to drive Ronnie to the rink? What d'you think he did while he waited for the game to end?

ROSE He used to help coach the peewees.

MURIEL Ronnie'll tell you – ask him.

ROSE Yes, I will.

MURIEL [*Contritely.*] Ach – we can't know more than a quarter of a person can we?

ROSE I knew that man. I lived with him for thirty years. [*Pause.*]

123

MURIEL Did you know about the cockfights?

ROSE He was a fine man.

MURIEL On Wednesday nights. When you were at the Ladies' Auxiliary ...

ROSE On Wednesdays ... I ...

MURIEL Well everyone else knew. They used to come to our place in droves. It was all very fast. Very hush-hush.

ROSE I think I will make that chowder tonight. [ROSE *brings a bucket in from the porch.*]

MURIEL No. Put some corn meal in with them. Let them stand overnight and flush themselves out. [*Pause.*] Ronnie and I were lookouts. Ronnie by the phone, me at the end of the lane. He used to give us a dollar each. We called it 'mum-money.' [ROSE *gives her a challenging glance.* MURIEL *puts her finger to her lips.* ROSE *shakes her head, denying it.*] I snuck away once. Ran over the fields and watched ... on the edge of the crowd – couldn't see much. A lot of money changing hands and him standing there in the middle holding the cock. He put its head in his mouth, I remember that, blowing down its throat, then a great fluttering of wings. Then it was all over.

ROSE You shouldn't have been watching. Cockfighting's illegal.

MURIEL One night the RCMP came 'round.

ROSE If he'd been caught ...

MURIEL Well, he never was.

ROSE I used to dread Wednesdays.

MURIEL You knew?

ROSE I lived with him.

MURIEL Well why didn't you ...?

ROSE No. [*Long pause.* ROSE *looks nervously at the door.*] Don't you say a word about this to Chuck. Do you hear me?

MURIEL Oh he was probably up in the field with the rest of them.

ROSE He knew your father by reputation. [MURIEL *looks at* ROSE *considering.*] I ... I've been wanting to talk. That's why I came a day early but you haven't had a minute.

MURIEL About Dad?

ROSE No, not that. We haven't even worked out the sleeping arrangements.

MURIEL Oh, you can take the double bed.

ROSE I hadn't realized the place was so small.

MURIEL We'll make out.

ROSE No. That is ... it isn't that kind of relationship. Not yet....
We'd be ... It wouldn't be suitable.

MURIEL Well, I'll sleep in the double with you – he can have this
bed out here.

ROSE It's not very comfortable.

MURIEL What do you want – a four-poster?

ROSE Well ... he might be ... I don't want him to think there's
anything funny – you and me – in your bed.

MURIEL [*Bursts out laughing.*] You can't be serious!

ROSE Well, he's bound to notice that you're ...

MURIEL [*Cuts in.*] I? I'm what?

ROSE You're not married.

MURIEL Does he judge women on their marital status? Sounds
like a typical banker.

ROSE Just a man that's all. He might not understand.

MURIEL [*Huffily.*] Can't say I do either.

ROSE Well ... [MURIEL *turns away brusquely.*] It's just that ...
he's very conventional. Most people are, aren't they?
His family had money. They lost it all in the Depression.

MURIEL He can always stay at the lodge.

ROSE No. I couldn't ask him to do that. Not after his daughter
was so kind. She gave me a room of my own.

MURIEL His married daughter – yes.

ROSE Yes. [MURIEL *works.* ROSE *waits expectantly.*]

MURIEL So I give up my room to Chuck and sleep in the barn? Is
that the idea?

ROSE Oh, would you?

MURIEL No I damned well ... [*Softening.*] Is it that important?

ROSE You think I'm stupid.

MURIEL Jesus!

ROSE You've gotta listen to me. It's been five years. A lot of
things've changed since your father's funeral –

MURIEL [*Looks up with sudden decision.*] You know ... You know
... I used to think you needed me. I stuck around longer
than I wanted to because ... I thought he used you and
you needed me as a buffer against him. And now I find

125

out that even that was a sham – that you knew all the time. You probably even knew about his shenanigans with Maggie Butler.

ROSE He was always a wild man. If you marry a wild man you take the consequences.

MURIEL He hated women.

ROSE No! He was proud of you.

MURIEL Proud! [MURIEL *gets up to look for a tool.* ROSE *watches her apprehensively.*]

ROSE We both were. 'Specially the way you handled those pigs. He cut that article out of the *Farmer's Gazette*. The one they wrote up about you and that other girl running the farm. What was her name?

MURIEL Barbara.

ROSE That's right. He pinned it up on the notice board outside the church hall. He was always stopping people and pointing it out. Finally the rector pinned another notice over the top of it. Your dad was mad as a bull. Tore the whole board down. We had to pay for another. Whatever happened to Barbara?

MURIEL I told you I'd make it alone. Well I have, haven't I? I ran a business – I got this place together and now I'm going to build the best goddamn house on the island. On my own. To my own design.

ROSE You can't isolate yourself. We all need other people.

MURIEL Look Mum – I'll try to explain. [*Goes over and sits beside* ROSE.] I don't mean to be hard. I just have to protect myself. I have to do things my way. Without interference from outside.

ROSE No man is an island.

MURIEL I'm a woman! [ROSE *stares at* MURIEL, *startled by her vehemence. She's about to retort when* MURIEL *silences her.*] A few months ago something happened here. It ... it kind of threw me for a while. Made me sit down and reconsider – you know – take a look at what I really wanted out of life.

ROSE What happened?

MURIEL [*Ignores the question.*] I looked around here ... tried to take stock of the old place. I began to see ... how ... how unfocused I'd allowed myself to get. I'd started clearing

a couple of spots, got a few head of stock, couple of
hens, weatherproofed part of the barn, made a half-
assed attempt at rewiring. Nothing carried through. I'd
let myself get sloppy. [*Waits for a response.*] I took too
much notice of other people. My first thought was to
modernize. So I got the place wired professionally, got a
new radio, a TV. Started watching a few news programs.
I almost wish I hadn't bothered. [*Nods at TV.*] You only
have to watch that thing for half an hour to see that it's
so fucking corrupt out there that you can't even trust
your neighbour any more. I began to see it all in
perspective. Not just my life but all the rest. On this
island, in Canada, in every developed country. We're all
being forced into living alone – being alone – don't you
see? Relationships don't make sense any more.

ROSE   You don't know what you're talking about –

MURIEL   I'm going to work up a business on my own. On a really
big scale. See here – here's the outline [*Points to wall
chart.*] I've got it all planned. I should have the
foundations of the house in by June. I figure that by
December I'll be clear enough to make a start on the
greenhouses. If I get a good run at it ... not too much
rain.

ROSE   It's all work – hard work. All work and no play ...

MURIEL   D'you know anything about hydroponics?

ROSE   Hydro ...?

MURIEL   You know – growing without soil.

ROSE   Not even soil!

MURIEL   It's chancy, but I'm going to give it a go. Next year ... next
year I'm going to work my ass off, Mum. I don't care if it
takes ten years.

ROSE   I'll bet there's a dozen good men who'd come here on
an hour's notice if you'd only give them half a chance.

MURIEL   It'll run itself. No need for men.

ROSE   What if something happened to you? You could lie in a
ditch for days –

MURIEL   Nothing's gonna happen to me –

ROSE   Nobody works just for themselves.

MURIEL   Working's what I do best. I had a good teacher.

ROSE   Me?

127

MURIEL   Whenever you turn on the radio every other song's about love and togetherness, and meanwhile everyone's freaking out –

ROSE   There's nothing wrong with togetherness.

MURIEL   And there's nothing wrong with aloneness either. If the politicians will ever allow it to happen.

ROSE   [*Relieved.*] Oh – that's what it's all about – politics are crazy anyway.

MURIEL   You can't have a political system that's built up on single isolated entities. Politicians depend on mass sentiment. You know, if they were really interested in our well-being they'd be educating us to live alone. But they daren't. They'd rather see us freak out. It's unacceptable isn't it? A woman on her own – making it without help from the system. Do they still makes jokes about spinsters back home?

ROSE   Look at Miss Arbuthnott. There's a spinster for you. D'you know she's still cleaning the school and the church hall?

MURIEL   Maybe she'll get her due one of these days.

ROSE   Oh we appreciate her efforts I'm sure. [*Laughs.*]

MURIEL   The gradual breakdown of all the groups we've ever known – the family, the church ... There aren't any precedents ... no one has anything to believe in any more – and if they're not allowed to believe in themselves then ...

ROSE   I worry about you.

MURIEL   Don't. I feel ... I feel ... centred for the first time in years.

ROSE   Yes. Self-centred. [MURIEL *gets up and goes over to her work.*] Ronnie's been good to me. They've shared their family – the kids. Never made me feel unwelcome.

MURIEL   I should think not – it's your house they're living in.

ROSE   Our house ... the family farm. [*Pause.*] They never make me feel in the way. It's me. [*Pause.*] I guess I need a man of my own.

MURIEL   Well you've found one so everything's dandy isn't it?

ROSE   Yes. [*Suddenly.*] I'm in love you know. [MURIEL *fits the sides of the desk together and bashes them into place loudly.*] All I wish is that you could feel the same way.

MURIEL   About Chuck? Most unlikely. Let's be quiet for a while, shall we?

ROSE   I don't like you to be ... bitter.

MURIEL   I'm happy. I'm real happy, Mum. That's all I was trying to say. Let's not talk, eh?

ROSE   Well you don't sound happy. [ROSE *gets up and goes to the stove. She glances at the time, then looks in the pot.*] It's going to be spoilt if he doesn't get here soon. [MURIEL *works, shutting* ROSE *out.* ROSE *wanders around the room, nervously rearranging flowers and she finally bursts out* ...] Chuck and I have been talking things over. [*She waits. No move from* MURIEL.] We thought we'd maybe get a boat and cruise around a bit. [*Pause.*] Oh, not like yours. Fibreglass – a big one. They're the latest thing. We'd maybe take a trip to Hawaii.

MURIEL   [*Without looking up.*] Alberta to Hawaii? Must be some boat!

ROSE   [*Quickly.*] We could keep her on our dock. [MURIEL *looks up sharply.*] The dock we'll build on the piece of property we're going to buy. If we like the island, of course. Well I know he'll like the island. There's nothing to keep us at home any more. Not now we're retired.

MURIEL   Wait a minute. Have I got this right? No, I didn't hear it.

ROSE   There's nothing settled yet. [MURIEL *forces the pieces of the desk together.*] Don't do that. Not now. I felt ... I felt we'd like to be closer. We'd like to be a family again. Ronnie and the kids can come out here in the winter – he likes to get away in winter. We can all be together.

MURIEL   [*Holding on to the pieces.*] Property prices are astronomical. Water front – do you know what you're looking at?

ROSE   Your father didn't leave me a pauper.

MURIEL   But that money's tied up in the farm, isn't it?

ROSE   We can always sell off a quarter-section.

MURIEL   What does Ronnie think of that?

ROSE   I haven't told him. Between you and me I'm worried about Ronnie. He never really wanted to be a farmer. I can see that now.

MURIEL   [*Laughs.*] You never used to listen when he told you that.

ROSE Well, I guess we knew. Your father always used to say that the blood got mixed up. You were the oldest and you should have been the boy, then it would all have worked out. As it was ...

MURIEL As it was he sent me off to do an arts degree and when it came to the crunch, you went along with him.

ROSE I didn't want you to ruin your life. I wanted you to grow into a ... a woman.

MURIEL [Indicating pieces of desk.] Here – hold this while I look for the clamps.

ROSE [Ignoring the request.] Yes. A woman. I wanted you to have children. [She goes over and takes hold of the desk.] Chuck says you're competing with your father. He says it's more common with boys but it can happen with girls.

MURIEL Who are you marrying, Sigmund Freud?

ROSE We mustn't quarrel. I know I have to learn to accept what you're doing.

MURIEL That's not necessary. Stop compromising yourself.

ROSE We all have to make compromises.

MURIEL Like this. [MURIEL corrects the way ROSE is holding the desk, walks away.] Where did I put those clamps?

ROSE Chuck says it'd be a good thing to make a clean break with the prairies.

MURIEL On my doorstep!

ROSE We mustn't let him see us quarrelling. [MURIEL, still searching, finds a handful of mail over the sink.]

MURIEL Oh – did you clear the mailbox?

ROSE Your father was always talking about retiring to the coast. [MURIEL goes through the mail.] You're gonna like Chuck.

MURIEL Look, Mum. I don't give a good goddamn about Chuck. I don't care whether I like him. It doesn't make any difference to me. Don't you understand?

ROSE His daughter took it very well – I warned him – I warned him that you were different.

MURIEL There's a package for me at the post office – I'll have to pick it up.

ROSE You hadn't emptied that mailbox in a week or more.

MURIEL Bills. Just bills. Who cares?

ROSE There's a letter there.

MURIEL [*Having seen it.*] Is there?

ROSE Aren't you going to open it?

MURIEL I guess so. Not right now. [ROSE *looks at her very closely.* MURIEL *turns away, mock-casual.*] What was I looking for?

ROSE I'd have come out here years ago. Before I even met him. It was just that ... I didn't know. I didn't know whether I'd be welcome. I just wasn't sure what was going on.

MURIEL I thought I'd made it clear. [MURIEL *goes to the screen door and begins to unscrew the hinge.*]

ROSE What are you doing?

MURIEL I have to fix this screen. There's a hole in it.

ROSE You were looking for the clamps.

MURIEL Oh yes. Yes. [MURIEL *looks around ineffectually, turns back to the door.*] When you're working on something big the little things get forgotten – this door ... [MURIEL *leaves the door. Wanders ineffectually around the room, looking for the clamps.*] Just hold onto that a bit longer, will you? I want to get this off. [*Begins to unscrew the hinge.* ROSE *watches* MURIEL *silently.* ALLI *comes onto the porch. Taps* MURIEL *on the shoulder.* MURIEL *jumps. Stiffens.* ALLI *walks past her into the room. She is carrying a bag and seems somewhat glazed and lifeless. She stops at the sight of* ROSE.]

ALLI Oh. Oh, I'm sorry. I didn't know you had company.

MURIEL [*Without moving.*] Alicia, this is my mother ... Mum ... [ROSE *indicates that she cannot leave the desk she is holding.*]

ALLI [*Smiling.*] Mrs. ...

ROSE [*Cuts* ALLI *short.*] Rose.

MURIEL Well ... [*At a loss.*] Aren't you going to put it down? [*Points to* ALLI's *bag.*]

ALLI [*Not moving.*] I walked up from the ferry.

MURIEL You must be exhausted.

ALLI No. I have lots of energy.

ROSE You didn't see anyone else? Anyone coming in this direction?

ALLI [*Looks at* MURIEL *quizzically.*] Were you expecting someone?

131

MURIEL Why didn't you let me know? ... [MURIEL *looks involuntarily at the letter.* ALLI *follows her look.*]

ALLI I called as well.

MURIEL I was probably outside.

ALLI Somebody answered. They asked me who I was. I said I was Alli. They said ...

MURIEL [*To* ROSE.] When was this? Why didn't you tell me?

ALLI Yesterday.

ROSE Just after I got here. I didn't think it was important ... I forgot about it in the excitement.

ALLI I wondered whether I should come, and then ... [*Shrugs.*]

MURIEL [*Trying to sound genuine.*] Well I'm glad you came.

ALLI You're surprised.

MURIEL Yeah. Yeah, sure I'm surprised. A nice surprise. Alli's an old friend, Mum. A close friend. Haven't seen her in six months. Not since ... We had an awful time with a calf and Alli split.

ALLI Who were you expecting?

MURIEL A friend of my mother's.

ALLI [*To* ROSE.] You're from Alberta, Rose?

ROSE Yes.

ALLI What's this? [ALLI *looks at the desk, which* ROSE *is still holding.*] A pulpit? Who's the preacher? [ROSE *lets go the desk. It falls apart.*] Are you going to live here now?

ROSE [*To* MURIEL.] I'm sorry.

MURIEL She's here on a visit.

ALLI [*Glancing at blueprints, puts on a preacher's voice.*] In my father's house are many mansions. [ROSE *moves to pick up the pieces.* MURIEL *pushes her aside, picks them up, and stacks them against the wall.*] [*To* ROSE.] We have quite a lot in common. [*Pause.*] We both have children. A boy and a girl.

ROSE Oh really? I didn't know.

ALLI Yes. Mine are called Denny and Christine. Christine's just had her seventeenth birthday. She's an Aries.

ROSE Oh?

ALLI Yes. Yours are called Muriel and Ronnie.

ROSE That's right.

ALLI Yes. She's getting quite grown up now. I haven't seen

132

her for a while. Not for ... oh ... not for eighteen months. Not since I came to live here. I wonder if I'd recognize her. [*Pause.*] You're not the way I thought.

MURIEL Why don't you take your coat off, Alli?

ALLI Alicia. You called me Alicia. [*To* ROSE.] No – I thought you'd be a bit of an old cow. You're not.

ROSE Well maybe I should leave you two together.

MURIEL Oh no. You don't have to go out. She didn't mean anything. [MURIEL *raises her voice awkwardly, unsure whether she is getting through to* ALLI.] Mum's staying here, Alli, her fiancé's coming tonight.

ALLI Don't shout, I'm not deaf. [*To* ROSE.] Well, we don't have so much in common after all.

ROSE Pardon?

ALLI My children were born in wedlock.

MURIEL My father died, Alli. Remember? Mum's getting married again. To a bank teller.

ROSE He's not –

MURIEL An ex-teller.

ROSE He was assistant manager.

ALLI Oh? My husband was a veterinarian.

ROSE Oh yes?

ALLI Yes. Karl.

MURIEL Alli was married for eighteen years.

ALLI [*To* ROSE.] I must tell you about it some time.

MURIEL Well – how've you been anyway?

ALLI Oh – well, very well. Yes. They're very pleased with me. I've made progress. Three gold stars. [*To* ROSE.] She still finishes off sentences with anyway. Does it run in the family?

MURIEL Alli's been in hospital, Mum.

ALLI In the nuthouse actually. [*Smiles.*] They taught me to be honest.

ROSE That's very unfortunate. Getting sick I mean.

ALLI They said I should express whatever I have on my mind. They said that most sickness is caused by repressing one's natural feelings. [*To* ROSE.] Do you agree with that?

ROSE I'm not an expert in that sort of –

ALLI [*Not listening.*] We spent most days practising.

Sometimes we did it in groups. Sometimes one-to-one. We were allowed to hit each other if we felt like it. I knocked an old lady out. Cold. With a chair. She irritated me you see. I didn't have to apologize because I was sick. She kept talking to herself. [*Pause.*] What was it she used to say? [ALLI *gets up and begins to pace up and down, thinking.* ROSE *and* MURIEL *watch, bewildered.* MURIEL *makes a movement to try to distract* ROSE's *attention.*] She kept pulling her hair out so they shaved the top of her head – bald as a soda cracker. And a fringe 'round the back. Very becoming. One of the other nutcases kept asking her how come she'd grown out of the top of her head? She'd say ... 'I never answer personal questions.' And all the time she went 'round muttering, 'I'm an unmarried lady of moderate means.' [ALLI *repeats the phrase over with many different emphases.* ROSE *and* MURIEL *begin to speak over the repeated phrase.*[

ROSE Is she all right?

MURIEL Of course she is.

ROSE But ...

MURIEL She does this occasionally. Meditates. I always thought of it as meditating.

ROSE I thought you sat still and played with beads when you did that.

MURIEL Oh, there are different ways. Some people stand on their heads.

ROSE What's she saying?

ALLI [*Suddenly addresses them aloud.*] I'm an unmarried lady of moderate means.

MURIEL A mantra.

ALLI It's all right. I don't need to work things out any more. I'm cured. I really don't have to talk to myself. [*To* ROSE.] I'm not dead. [*To* MURIEL.] And it isn't a mantra. [*Looks at* MURIEL *closely.*] You're not very pleased about the bank teller, are you?

MURIEL Of course I am. It's just that – [*Stops short.* ALLI *and* ROSE *wait for her to continue. Blurts out.*] They're thinking of moving out here to the island. Aren't you, Mum?

ROSE Well we ...

ALLI Oh? [*Laughs, to* MURIEL.] Have you told her?

MURIEL There's nothing to tell.

ALLI You used to think there was. Don't you remember ...? [*Sings.*] 'If she could see us now ...' [*Looks at* MURIEL's *frightened face.*] No? [*Takes a breath, turns to* ROSE.] The hospital was on the mainland. A long way away.

ROSE And now you're better.

MURIEL Alli, look –

ALLI Yes. Better.

MURIEL For heaven's sake put your bag down. [*Gets glasses and a bottle.*]

ALLI Well, I don't want to inconvenience ... No, that's not true. [*Puts bag down, takes her coat off.*] I don't mind inconveniencing you at all.

MURIEL Did they give you pills? [MURIEL *pours drinks. She gives one to* ROSE.]

ALLI Oh yes. [*Scrabbles in her bag.*] Look. [*Lays out some containers.*] These take me up, and these bring me down if I've gone too far, and these make me pee because the others inhibit the bladder. Then I've got some more in case I pee too much ... [ALLI *takes a pill.* MURIEL *gets her a glass of water.*]

MURIEL Should you drink? [*Puts* ALLI's *drink aside.*]

ALLI Oh come on. Don't be a spoilsport. [MURIEL *pours* ALLI *a drink.*]

ROSE Not so much, Muriel.

ALLI [*To* ROSE.] I can tell that you're a very good mother. [*Pause.* ROSE *and* MURIEL *exchange looks.*] I wasn't. I was a lousy mother. Terrible. Terrible.

MURIEL That's nonsense. You were a marvellous mother. [*To* ROSE.] The kids adored her.

ALLI Denny came to see me. Christine didn't. He's learning to play the guitar. He brought it with him. Electric. Everything's electric these days. [*Looks up at light.*]

ROSE Is he musical?

ALLI I don't think so. It took two male nurses to carry in the equipment. He sat and played all afternoon. It saved having to talk, you see. Two of the inmates flipped out. Oh, this wasn't the clinic where I was before. This was the hospital. Public. The patients weren't genteel. When

they flipped, they flipped. Denny was asked to leave. No,
I don't think he's musical.

ROSE I'll make a cup of tea.

ALLI We always drink coffee.

MURIEL Tea's okay.

ROSE I'd offer you something to eat but ... but I don't think
there's enough. Maybe you can get something at the
lodge. [ALLI *ignores this. She gets up, flicks the light on
and off.*]

ALLI She was always threatening to electrify the place ... but
there was plenty of electricity around in those days. We
were all wired up. [ALLI *sits and looks at* MURIEL. *A long
pause.* MURIEL *puts out her hand and touches* ALLI
*reassuringly, checking first to see that her mother's back
is turned. She puts her fingers to her lips, warning.*]
When I came out they sent me to stay with Karl's sister
Stella. She's a skydiver. She's very long-suffering – it's
brought on by high altitudes. [*Karl's voice.*] 'One of these
days Stella will really come down to earth.' She did.
When I arrived. She was glad when I left. She kept
saying things like ... 'You're going to have to stand on
your own two feet, Alicia.' As if I was levitating or
something.

ROSE Where's the pot?

MURIEL There. [MURIEL *points. The teapot is full of flowers.*]

ROSE Is this the only one you have?

ALLI [*Refers to flowers.*] Who died? [ROSE *picks up the flowers
and puts them all outside.*]

MURIEL You didn't have to do that.

ALLI Oh. They're for the financé. [*To* ROSE.] You know you're
lucky to get a second go. At your age.

MURIEL Alli, that's obnoxious!

ROSE No it's not. [*Comes up to* ALLI, *speaks simply.*] Yes, you're
quite right. I do consider myself lucky. I'm a lucky
woman. [*Goes over, tests the phone.*]

MURIEL There's nothing wrong with the line. [ROSE *goes to the
stove. She takes the pot of food off.*]

ALLI I'll bet she can cook like a dream.

MURIEL Of course she can. She makes a mean clam chowder.

ROSE [*Not to be patronized.*] You said it took your fillings out.

MURIEL I got the new stove hooked up. That way I don't need to light the fire in the summer.

ALLI You shouldn't have done it. Not for me.

MURIEL I didn't.

ALLI No?

MURIEL No. No. Not for you.

ALLI For somebody else?

MURIEL I bought it for myself.

ALLI Hoping I'd come back and get you organized.

MURIEL No.

ALLI Well, I'm here. [*Picks up the frying pan.*] Lead me to it. [ALLI *lifts the lid on the pot, sniffs, laughs. Tosses the frying pan over her shoulder. She looks at the grave faces watching her. She speaks to* MURIEL, *nodding at* ROSE.] You're like her. Or is she like you? I can see the resemblance.

ROSE Oh, people always used to say she was like her father.

ALLI Is that so? Yes, I guess she would be. I wonder if Christine's going to be like me? Poor kid.

MURIEL Why don't you call her up and talk to her?

ALLI Oh no ... no. I can't do that. Supposing I got Karl on the line? [*Karl's voice.*] 'I'm afraid she's out to lunch, Alicia. Out to lunch. Like her mother.' [*To* ROSE.] You must forgive me for talking so much, I can't help it. It's known as a pathological necessity in the trade.

MURIEL I could call. Why don't I do it now? Would you like to speak with her? Karl won't recognize my voice. [*Goes to the phone.*]

ROSE We should keep the line open.

ALLI [*Overlaps* ROSE, *agitated.*] Oh no. No. Don't do that.

MURIEL All right!

ALLI Don't shout!

MURIEL Calm down.

ALLI He's suing for divorce. Mental cruelty. He wants custody of the children.

ROSE [*Sitting down at the table.*] The water takes forever to boil on this stove.
[*Pause.*]

ALLI You haven't been concentrating, Muriel.

MURIEL What?

ALLI Everything seems sort of scattered. You're getting as bad as me.

MURIEL Not normally.

ALLI Where are the dogs?

ROSE Yes – I'm surprised you haven't got a dog Muriel.

MURIEL Oh, they're around somewhere.

ALLI [*Gets up.*] No they're not.

MURIEL Where are you proposing to stay tonight?

ALLI Oh, it's okay. I can sleep in here. [ALLI *indicates the bedroom. She walks over and goes through the door into the bedroom.* MURIEL *and* ROSE *exchange looks.*]

MURIEL My mother's sleeping in ...

ALLI [*Comes out.*] The bed looks bare. It needs a quilt.

MURIEL Quilt?

ALLI Yes. [*To* ROSE.] We never had one. We used the old dog blanket instead. The dogs were always on the bed. I made this quilt, you see. For Muriel.

ROSE That was very kind of you.

ALLI I'm not a very good needlewoman. [*Pause.*] I made it in the hospital. [*She takes the quilt out of her bag. She has nothing else in it. The quilt is half-finished, full of holes.*] And where are the fucking dogs?

MURIEL [*Not touching the quilt.*] I gave them away.

ROSE You ...?

MURIEL Yes. I decided to get rid of all the animals. Mostly to the neighbours. I had some of them put down.

ALLI [*Picks up the quilt.*] Shall I put it on the bed?

ROSE But you love dogs. [MURIEL *shrugs.*] Ever since you were a little girl. You always had a dog. Don't you remember Aida? [ALLI *bursts out laughing.*] Be quiet! Be quiet, can't you? Well if you're going to live alone at least you should have a dog.

ALLI It's such a funny name for a dog. [ALLI *wraps the quilt around her like an African sarong, beats her chest.*]

ALLI [*Bass voice.*] I ... Eda. Who you?

ROSE Look. I don't know who you are but –

MURIEL [*Warning.*] Mum!

ROSE She used to like opera. We used to listen to it on the radio on Saturday afternoons. The men had no time for it. [*To* MURIEL.] I know you used to like it ...

MURIEL Yes. I did. I do.

ALLI I didn't know that. You never sang me any arias.

MURIEL God, Alli. I didn't have to tell you everything.

ALLI Why not? Why not? We lived together didn't we? Aren't we supposed to confide in each other? [*Sings, from Faust.*] 'All hail though dwelling pure and lowly. All hail thou dwelling pure and lowly ...' Go on – your turn – remember the singing game? Try Faust ...

MURIEL You haven't changed a bit have you? You're a wrecker, Alli. A wrecker.

ALLI You can't wreck what's already ... [*Tails off, turns away. ROSE gets up and pours water into the teapot.*] I don't think the water was boiling.

MURIEL It's not convenient for you to stay here right now. I'll drive you down to the lodge and get you a room for a couple of nights till you've figured out what you want to do. I'll meet you there tommorow. If I'd known I'd have ...

ALLI What? What would you have done?

ROSE Yes. It think you should go. We're expecting someone.

ALLI What's she doing in our home?

ROSE You're upsetting my daughter.

ALLI Upsetting your daughter? Your daughter's calm. Made out of steel, your daughter. She's got a smile like a steel trap. Always damn well in control. Everything under control. Where was I? Oh yes – after I left Stella's I went to stay in a hotel on Hastings Street.

MURIEL [*Horrified.*] Hastings Street? Are you mad?

ALLI Yes.

MURIEL Hastings Street!

ALLI I left after a week. I couldn't pay the rent. I took a job as a chambermaid in another hotel.

MURIEL Alli, how could you?

ALLI I was fired. For smoking in the laundry closet.

MURIEL You don't smoke.

ALLI Maybe I was trying to burn the goddamn place down.

ROSE You ... what? Muriel, she's ... dangerous.

ALLI She never came to see me, your daughter. Not once. She was too busy. Too much to do. The hospital was a long way away – on the far side of town. It took a fair chunk out of her day. It wasn't as far as the nursing home where she met me – she came every day then. She was supposed to be visiting her live-in. But her live-in was living out. There was no hammock in the hospital. No lawn. Only a concrete parking lot.

MURIEL I'm sorry.

ALLI It doesn't matter now, I'm home. [*They all stare at each other.*] Do you know what they did to me?

MURIEL Not here. Not now.

ALLI [*To* ROSE.] They tie you down, you know.

MURIEL It was your choice. The whole thing was ... We all make our own choices.

ALLI They had to get my husband's permission. I told them that you were my next of kin, but they said that was impossible. They put a rubber gag in your mouth. Your whole body ... turns to water.

MURIEL Alli – [MURIEL *puts her arms around* ALLI, *anguished. They embrace and cling to each other. To* ROSE.] Don't stare. Don't stare at us. [ROSE *gets up.*] If you hadn't come here ... you can't go on keeping things quiet.

ROSE Why not? Tell me why not?

MURIEL It isn't honest, that's why.

ROSE Honesty!

MURIEL Tell her Alli. Go on. Tell her what we used to do in that bed. [*Breaks away from* ALLI; *to* ROSE.] Well, don't tell me you didn't know. You who knows everything.

ROSE I don't have to have my nose rubbed in it to know that.... All that talk about being on your own. It wasn't anything to do with it. I was just ... just ... you couldn't come out and tell me I was in the way.

MURIEL Why do you have to interfere – all of you?

ROSE I should've interfered long ago. [MURIEL *and* ROSE *face each other.*] Yes.

MURIEL Tell me I'm a freak then. Unnatural ... [ROSE *slaps her suddenly, sharply.* ALLI *moves over to* MURIEL. MURIEL *pushes them both away.*]

ALLI Muriel and I ...

MURIEL [*Turns on* ALLI *suddenly.*] I don't want to hurt you. I don't want to hurt either of you ... Oh God! [MURIEL *stands immobile, caught between the two, who move in on her.*]

ALLI [*Stretches out her hand.*] Muriel, I ...

ROSE Get away from her!

ALLI Muriel.

ROSE Muriel!

ALLI Listen! [MURIEL *cries out and rushes into the yard. The two women stare at each other for a moment. ROSE goes to the door, undecided whether to follow. ALLI wanders around the room, aimlessly.*] They asked me a lot of questions in the hospital. They were always asking me questions. The wrong questions. I always gave them the answers. They were always patient. Always tactful and understanding. They wrote down all the answers. It must have made boring reading. 'Do you think you're a lesbian, Mrs. Delgiudice?' Cold storage. 'What about your husband?' Cold storage. 'Were you on good terms – socially?' Cold storage. 'Sexually?' Cold storage. 'Do you believe in God?' Cold storage. I knew what they really wanted to know. [*Leans forward, speaks confidingly.*] 'Why did you lose your mind Alli?' [*Pause.*] I didn't *lose* my mind – I just put it away for a while. In cold storage. I had a question, too. 'Why are you using so many words, why don't you just shut up and listen?' [*Pause.*] I listened tonight. I listened as soon as I walked off the ferry. Even before. I stood in the barn and listened. There was no smell of dung – no bales of hay. The moment I walked into the yard I knew. The silence answered my question. I knew I'd made a mistake. [ROSE *sits down, she is listening to* ALLI *now.*] They made their diagnosis on cold storage. Paranoid schizophrenic symptoms, diminished responses possibly due to childhood trauma, manifold inhibitions ... etcetera, etcetera. Prognosis – uncertain. [*Pause.*] After they let me out of the hospital I met a listener. In the Only Café, on Hastings Street. The name is a fraud. There are dozens of cafés on Hastings Street, but the Only is the only café with a seahorse outside that winks. She was sitting in a booth, the listener, falling asleep over her fried herring. A native person. Isn't that what you're supposed to call them? Native persons – they're not Indians any more. There were two guys sitting at the

counter. I sat down in the booth and watched her
eyelids twitch as she started to snore. I watched her
listening to the dreams as they flicked across her face.
Listening to the past. It was a young face but it looked
very old. She had a bottle tucked between her breasts,
under her blouse, with the neck sticking out ... and she
kept stroking it as if it were a baby, or ... or a lover. [*She
makes a stroking motion, turns away from the door and
leans forward, as if watching.*] She's very thin. [*Faster.*]
Suddenly one of the guys leans across and pulls the
bottle out – but he doesn't make it. She's awake in a
second and she grabs the bottle and brings it down on
his fingers. It smashes against the table. Blood and rye
and no more smell of herring. And he yells, 'You know
what you are? You're a man with a cunt. A man with a
frigging cunt.' She doesn't say a word. Just listens.
[*Pause.*] They leave. I lean across. I want her to listen to
me you see. I want her to listen – but I've forgotten how
to make her hear. She starts to eat the fish. Very
delicately, dainty little piles, fish on one side, bones on
the other. No fuss. [*Pause.*] I wanted to touch her, I
wanted to feel what it was like to be that bottle, to come
out of cold storage. She was so much herself. Like
Muriel. I wanted to talk to her, but the head of the
herring was staring at me. So I said to her. 'Would you
mind removing the head?' And she picks it up and puts
it between two pieces and bread and hands it to me. A
present? I don't know. I'm not listening hard enough.
Maybe she thinks I'm funny. I close my eyes and I bite
into it. I don't know how long it takes to chew but when
I open my eyes again she's fallen asleep. The face
doesn't move now, absolutely still, like a frozen
moccasin. I slip what's left of the sandwich into my
purse and get up out of the booth very quietly so as not
to wake her. I pay for my french fires with the coins in
my glove, and leave the Only Café with a smile on my
face. It isn't until I'm crossing Hastings Street that I look
in my purse and I notice that my change purse has
gone. My change purse and the diamond eternity ring

which was a present from my husband Karl on our
tenth wedding anniversary. I go back to the Only.

ROSE On Hastings Street?

ALLI [*Ignoring the interruption.*] She isn't there. Her plate's
still there and a pile of bones and the bottle on the floor
... but the flesh has gone and the native person has
disappeared. So thin. Maybe she's slipped down a crack
in the floor. Maybe I'm carrying her head in my purse. I
go over to the booth and I move the bones, and the
Chinese waiter comes up. 'I'm looking for a ring,' I say.
'Have you seen a diamond ring?' He shrugs and I get
down and start to look on the floor. He goes to the
counter and phones the police. I'm still on the floor
when they come, and I tell them I'm looking for eternity.
They take me to the Emergency in a truck with a
flashing light. [*Laughs.*] I never did like that ring anyway.
[*Pause.*] They tried to send me back to the hospital.
They wouldn't let me leave without giving an address. I
wanted to talk to Muriel. She was the only one who ever
listened. In the beginning she listened, before she ...
before I ... [*Gesture of helplessness.*] I told them I lived
on an island. On a farm on an island, with a woman.

ROSE Are you all right?

ALLI They're walking around, you know. All over town.

ROSE Who?

ALLI Questions.

ROSE I don't know the town. I only came to the coast once
before. With my husband. Just after Muriel was born.

ALLI She's looking for you.

ROSE No she's not. She's unloading the truck. Look!

ALLI Unloading?

ROSE Glass. She has glass on the back.
[*Pause.*]

ALLI Well – how does it feel? [ROSE *looks up, questioning.*]
Knowing.

ROSE What?

ALLI Knowing your daughter's a dyke. I don't know how I'd
feel if Christine ... I'd pretend to be very understanding
but ...

143

ROSE You disgust me.

ALLI [*Eagerly.*] Do I? Do I really?

ROSE I'm sorry. I don't know what made me say that. I know you can't help it.

ALLI What?

ROSE Chuck mustn't know. [*Gets up.*]

ALLI Chuck? Ah yes – Chuck. I wasn't listening. He's important.

ROSE [*Suddenly.*] Is Muriel sick?

ALLI Sick? You mean like me?

ROSE Well – what did I do? Where did I go wrong?

ALLI You're asking too many questions.

ROSE [*Tired.*] I don't know what you're trying to tell us.

ALLI You haven't been listening.

ROSE Are you making fun of me?

ALLI That's a good question.

ROSE Why? Why?

ALLI That's a bad question.

ROSE She doesn't approve of what I'm doing.

ALLI You're so serious. Like Muriel.
[*Pause.*]

ROSE You can't stay here, you know. She wants to be on her own. She's made that quite clear.

ALLI Then maybe we should leave her alone.

ROSE What's she doing out there?

ALLI Unloading the glass.

ROSE Then I can drive down and pick up Chuck. [ALLI *nods. Pause.*] Do you have any money?

ALLI No. [ROSE *puts a number of bills on the table.* ALLI *ignores the money.*]

ROSE Put it away. I don't want her to see it.

ALLI Why not? You're always covering up after everybody. Like a cat – you give it something it doesn't like and it tries to cover it up. That's why I hate cats. [*She sweeps the money to the floor.* ROSE *picks it up.*]

ROSE I was trying to do what's best. I ... I'd like to be able to understand. [*Pause.*] I hit her. [ALLI *laughs.*] I've never done that. Even when she was a little girl. [ALLI *starts to circle the floor, preoccupied.*] Where will you go? [ALLI *shrugs.*] I feel as though in some way she might have ... done you a disfavour.

ALLI [*Trying out the word.*] Disfavour? Dis-favour. [*Laughs.*] No.

ROSE I'm just ... sorry.

ALLI That's where Muriel gets it from. She's always sorry. [ROSE *reaches out her hand. The phone rings.* ROSE *bounds over and grabs it.*]

ROSE Oh, it's you. Where are you? Thank God. I was worried about you, dear. Stay right where you are – I'm coming to pick you up – I hope you're not too hungry. [*Pauses, listens, glances at the pot.*] Ten minutes – okay? [*Pause, embarrassed.*] I love you too. [ROSE *waits for him to ring off before replacing the receiver.*]

ALLI Mrs. Chuck. Not a bad choice, Mrs. Chuck. Do you think I'll like him?

ROSE Oh you won't meet ... [*Stops, looks at* ALLI.] He's a very simple man.

ALLI Shall we shake him up?

ROSE No! You? Yes, you would, wouldn't you?

ALLI He's not used to honesty?

ROSE I don't know. [*Long pause.*]

ALLI It's all right, you know. I'll stay out of the way if that's what you want.

ROSE We can't stay here. [MURIEL *enters.*]

MURIEL The truck's unloaded. [*To* ALLI.] I'll drive you down. ALLI *picks up her coat and bag.*]

ROSE Where's my case? [MURIEL, *surprised, indicates the bedroom.*] He called.

MURIEL Good.

ROSE Can I have the keys?

MURIEL Oh I was going to ... [*Gestures to* ALLI.]

ROSE No. I'll take him to the lodge and we'll get the morning ferry. [ROSE *goes through to the bedroom to pick up her things. Deep silence between* ALLI *and* MURIEL.]

MURIEL Well?

ALLI You needn't worry about your daughter Mrs. Chuck.

There'll always be someone for Muriel. [*Puts on her coat.*]

MURIEL Clear your head, Alli. [ALLI *puts the money in her pocket, slow motion.*]

ROSE [*Reenters with her case.*] Ready. [*To* ALLI.] You're coming with me? [ALLI *nods.* ROSE *bustles, collecting the last of her things.*] Be sure and get something to eat on the ferry. Just follow the sea road, right Muriel? Chuck's got himself as far as the store ... [*To* ALLI.] I'll drop you off. [*To* MURIEL.] I'll drive the truck back tomorrow, then maybe you'll be good enough to ...

MURIEL Yes. Come for breakfast.

ROSE Well then –

MURIEL I'm afraid I don't have any champagne. [*They embrace briefly.* ROSE *exits.* MURIEL *calls.*] The ferry leaves early. Make sure you don't sleep in.

[MURIEL *and* ALLI *pause, then throw their arms around each other. The truck starts up.* ALLI *leaves hurriedly.* MURIEL, *left alone, looks around, distracted. She finally picks up the quilt, looks at it closely, crosses slowly, puts it on the bed, and sits on it. She gets up and returns to her desk.*]

END

WAR BABIES

Notes

War Babies was first coproduced in a slightly different form by the New Play Centre, Vancouver, and the Belfry Theatre, Victoria, in January, 1984, with the following cast:

ESME CREARY *Nicole Lipman* BARBARA *Anna Hagan*
COLIN CREARY *Tim Koetting* PADDY *Anna Hagan*
TAILOR *Andrew Ball* Director: *James Roy*
JACK MACNEIL *Duncan Fraser*
    Characters:

ESME CREARY *A playwright, age 42.*
COLIN CREARY *Esme's husband, a newsman, age 42.*
ESME 2 *The character depicted by Esme in P.W.P.*
COLIN 2 *The character depicted by Colin in P.W.P.*
BARBARA *Around 40.*
JACK MACNEIL *Scottish, early 40's.*
CRAIG / JAILOR *Age 19. The identity of this character is not immediately evident to the audience.*
POLICEMAN 1 *Doubled by actor playing Jack.*
STORE CLERK *Doubled by actor playing jailor.*
PADDY *Doubled by actor playing Barbara.*

    The action of the play takes place in Colin and Esme's town house in a large eastern city. The bedroom should be on an upper level. For the P.W.P. scenes the apartment becomes in turn a jail, an auditorium, a bar, and a department store; the set should be able to accommodate these quick transformations and to provide the scope for the simultaneity of action which the script calls for.

Author's note: P.W.P. signified Play Within Play: these scenes may be marked in production by lighting changes; another possibility is to place all the fictional characters on the periphery of these scenes as they are being played.

    The word *beat* is used to indicate a break in the rhythm which is so swift as to allow no time for reflection. The word *pause* indicates that such time is allowed.

Act I, Scene One

The bedroom of COLIN *and* ESME's *House. Darkness. We hear the voices of* COLIN *and* ESME.

COLIN There's nobody else in here is there?

ESME Listen.

COLIN There is somebody!

ESME Yes?

COLIN I can hear breathing. [ESME *breathes deeply. Pause.*]

COLIN I don't know why we have to do it in the dark.

ESME So you won't cheat.

COLIN Well, it's easier to cheat in the dark. Am I being punished?

ESME No, silly.

COLIN Let's have some music.

ESME You have to stop while I put it on. How will I know you've stopped?

COLIN Put the light on.

ESME That'd be cheating. [*Beat.*] We'll do it together. Where are you?

COLIN Here.

ESME Take my hand. [*They grope their way to the tape deck.*] What do you want to hear?

COLIN Is there a choice?

ESME I left the Scarlatti here somewhere. Yes. [*She puts tape on. Music. A high-pitched childish voice sings 'Humpty Dumpty Sat On a Wall'. They laugh. Music stops.*]

COLIN Did you turn if off? [*They go back to their chairs. Silence.*]

ESME If you were blind ...

COLIN A blind rat caught in a wheel ... [*Loud bang.*]

COLIN [*Screams.*] Esme! Es ... what was that?

ESME I dropped a stitch.

COLIN Oh Jesus!

ESME Aren't you used to things that go bump in the night?

COLIN Round one.

ESME To me.

COLIN I'll get you next time!

ESME   Ssssh – I'm concentrating. [*Silence. Alarm clock goes off.*]

COLIN   That's it!

ESME   One more minute!

COLIN   No – that's it. Prize for the best.

    [*Lights come up. Late evening. They have both been knitting, and hold up the oddly shaped results of their efforts. They measure them one against the other.*]

ESME   How many stitches do you have left?

COLIN   [*Counts.*] I lost six.

ESME   I only lost three – I won.

COLIN   Mine's more perfect.

ESME   Mine's longer.

COLIN   Mines! [*Beat.*] Length wasn't the criterion.

ESME   It was understood.

COLIN   Not by me.

ESME   Understanding isn't your strong point.

COLIN   What's he going to do with two scarves?

ESME   She'll tie them together.

COLIN   He'll have perfect co-ordination?

ESME   Naturally. I thought of a name today. Sandra. D'you like Sandra?

COLIN   I prefer Matthew.

ESME   How about Matthew Sandra?

COLIN   Shouldn't we be making boots?

ESME   Too advanced. We need lesson two. [*Looks in book.*] How to read a pattern.

COLIN   Lesson three – knitting socks for soliders.

ESME   There's no war on.

COLIN   Perfect peace. [*Snores.*]

ESME   Maybe Barb'll show us when she gets here.

COLIN   Yeah – I'll bet she spends most of her time knitting when she's through with tossing the hay and whittling sticks.

ESME   That was back in the sixties. She can't still be a hippie. [*Laughs.*] She once crocheted a cover for her truck while she was waiting for the phone to ring. [*Looks through pattern book.*] You never called her. Well, she was your 'lady.'

COLIN   Lady?

ESME Today she'd be called your 'significant other,' right? [*Let's book drop.*]

COLIN Lesson four. How to be a single mother.

ESME We're in this together.

COLIN [*Knitting.*] Let's buy the bloody boots.

ESME If you want to learn to be a mother –

COLIN I'll learn it from you, when you've got the hang of it –

ESME Together.

COLIN Look – you don't have to keep feeding me tidbits to make me think I'm sitting at the table.

ESME Is that what you think?

COLIN I think you're trying to muzzle me.

ESME Then go ahead and bite! [*Beat.*] Listen – can't we can the war games?

COLIN What?

ESME Cant we make out without playing games? I mean – we're grown up mummies and daddies now. When the kid comes –

COLIN We'll roast him and feed him to the poor. You can write about it.

ESME Not such a *swift* idea – it's been down. [*Beat.*] I want you to be serious.

COLIN [*Straightens face, manually poses with her.*] The newsman and the playwright caught in a serious moment.

ESME We've got to make some adjustments.

COLIN [*Adjusts pose. ESME won't go along with it. COLIN gives up.*] Oh God – let's go over this when I get back.

ESME That's one of the adjustments. [*Beat.*] I don't think you should go away again. [*Beat.*] It might be early.

COLIN I'll be here to deliver – don't worry.

ESME I don't think you even want to.

COLIN Want to? Go ask the boys at the office – I'm boring them to tears on the subject. Russ Pringle even sent me a pacifier in the internal mail.

ESME I suppose that's an internal male joke!

COLIN Peace!

ESME Yes, that's it. Peace. You know, I sometimes dream there's a little replica of you [*points at his stomach*] in there – curled up with a gun.

COLIN [*Laughs.*] I don't have a gun.

ESME No?

COLIN I wouldn't bring a gun into the house –

ESME Have you ever used one?

COLIN No – of course not –

ESME But in your job –

COLIN I use a camera.

ESME Show me some of your pictures.

COLIN Sure.

ESME Now. Show me some of the ones you took in the Sudan.

COLIN Oh they have the whole file in Washington. You don't want to see them anyway –

ESME I do. How many newsmen get to testify in Washington!

COLIN It was nothing. I do it every day! [ESME *smiles. Hugs him.*] How many non-American newsmen!

ESME Wish I'd been there to see it. [COLIN *smiles and nods.*] Is it all desert?

COLIN Washington?

ESME The Sudan, silly. [COLIN *laughs.*] Supposing our pasts are stapled into our genes – yours and mine. [*Rubs belly reflectively.*] You know something? I feel like I'm starting out on some kind of a journey.

COLIN Make sure I'm on board.

ESME Oh yes.

COLIN What's the vehicle?

ESME A typewriter.

COLIN [*Looks at her oddly, then relaxes.*] Ach – let's get back into our cruising gear, Es. C'mon. [*Makes a grab for her but she gets up.*] Come back here. [*Pause.*] Sandra?

ESME [*Downstairs now, picks up newspaper. Calls up.*] You finished with this paper?

COLIN What paper?

ESME I haven't read it. [*She stands for a few moments deep in thought, looking at* COLIN *over the paper.*]
BLACKOUT.

Scene Two

We hear a radio playing. It is a talk show. Lights up on
ESME *and* COLIN *at the kitchen table. They are finishing*
lunch. COLIN *wears rugby shorts and shirt.*

ESME   More ice cream?

COLIN   No thanks.

ESME   All natural ingredients. [*Leans over and turns radio down*
to a background buzz, takes a drink of wine.] To us.

COLIN   To us.

ESME   If you really loved me you wouldn't let me drink, not in
my condition. [COLIN *obligingly takes her glass and*
finishes it. ESME *pours another drink for herself.*] Good
game?

COLIN   So so. We lost. [*Dabs his mouth with serviette.*] Whoops!
Another one for the wash.

ESME   Doesn't matter. [*Throws her serviette over her shoulder.*]

COLIN   You should use paper ones. Cut down on the work.

ESME   I like the work. [COLIN *looks at her closely.*] I do.

COLIN   You've been at it all morning. I can tell – this floor.

ESME   Scrubbed. On my hands and knees.

COLIN   You never scrub floors.

ESME   You should see what I found behind the fridge.

COLIN   You moved the fridge?

ESME   A condom.

COLIN   Esme you ... moved the fridge?

ESME   Did you hide it from me?

COLIN   You know I ...

ESME   Did you think I'd ask you to wear it? [*She looks at her*
stomach dubiously.]

COLIN   There's only another month – you know you mustn't
move heavy objects.

ESME   I blew it up. It floated.

COLIN   Es!

ESME   It's okay. I didn't feel a twinge. Won't do it again.
Promise. I went to the bank this morning. Opened an
account for the baby.

153

COLIN But he doesn't have a name.

ESME I opened it in the name of Bump. The teller recognized me from that quiz show on TV last month – how about that? I told her there's no way I'd get away with a hold-up in this city! She even asked about you – you see, you're a marked man too.

COLIN Bump?

ESME Bump Creary. Five bucks.

COLIN Here – make that fifty.

ESME Big spender!

COLIN It's worth it.

ESME [*Restless.*] Think I'll start on the den this afternoon.

COLIN No, not the den.

ESME Wonder what I'll find behind the desk?

COLIN Leave it to Mrs. Price.

ESME Oh – didn't I tell you? I fired her. She was reading our letters. [COLIN *sighs.*] The minute I decide to relax I see another cobweb, or an old sock, or ... do you think I have a problem?

COLIN Sounds to me like you're trying to make a goddamned nest.

ESME Am I?

COLIN You're reverting to the primitive.

ESME Is that why I fixed the dishwasher?

COLIN You?

ESME Well, you weren't going to do it. It was dripping.

COLIN You know my biggest fear? After this lot's over I'm gonna come home and I'm not gonna recognize my own wife. She'll metamorphose into some gigantic walking tit with a feather duster and a pair of pliers strapped round the nipple.

ESME All the better to tighten your nuts my love. [COLIN *hugs her.* ESME *pushes him away.*] You stink – you and your rugby.

COLIN We'll use paper cups and plates till ... It's not for much longer.

ESME Why is everything disposable?

COLIN It isn't. [*Beat.*]

ESME Anyway we can't use paper. Not with guests coming.

COLIN I knew it, that's why you're cleaning.

ESME It's not.

COLIN Let me put them off.

ESME They're on their way. The letter said they were heading down the west coast, then up the east and turning left at New York. Even Mrs. Price thought that sounded a bit vague.

COLIN I'll track them down – if I phone around one of the wire service boys'll ...

ESME Oh you and your 'boys.' Leave it Col. They're coming.

COLIN Why did you ask them?

ESME Haven't we been through this?
[*Silence.*]

COLIN Why do you keep putting me in the adversary role lately?

ESME Do I? How interesting.

COLIN Not for me.

ESME I want them here.

COLIN Well I don't.

ESME An extended family. [*She picks up her napkin, folds it neatly.*]

COLIN You're crazy.

ESME Are you still in love with Barb?

COLIN Oh don't be ... don't get onto that!

ESME You are!

COLIN She was just a girlfriend. [*Pause.*] I haven't seen her for fifteen years, love doesn't last that long.

ESME Is it disposable? [COLIN *turns off the radio.* ESME *folds his napkin.*]

COLIN And Jack? Am I supposed to stand by while he tells me what a wonderful father he's been to your kid.

ESME [*Flinches, covers.*] Well, you're best buddies.

COLIN Were. Fifteen years ago. And Barbara was supposed to be your best friend. I haven't noticed you straining to keep in touch with her.

ESME Maybe he'll have changed.

COLIN Jack? You know damned well he won't've changed. I'll bet he's going out of his mind there in frontierland. He'd give his eye teeth to be in my shoes.

ESME I can't see him wanting to be a father again. Imagine! My ex-husband – he'll be forty-two!

COLIN   I'm forty-two.

ESME   Yes, but you always did leave things to the last minute.

COLIN   Ouch!

ESME   You wish you'd been him!

COLIN   I do not.

ESME   Neither do I.

COLIN   I just don't want to talk about him that's all. He had the makings of a first-rate newsman – used to get all the plums. D'you know he broke the Six Day War? He was on the North America desk at Reuter and ... what's he doing now? Editing some two-bit rural rag!

ESME   You think he'll be jealous of you and your war games?

COLIN   Why did you ask them, Esme? [*Beat.*]

ESME   I was scared.

COLIN   Scared?

ESME   Scared you wouldn't be here.

COLIN   The likelihood's ... look – even if by some fluke I weren't here – we have friends. Close friends ...

ESME   But Barb and Jack are more than friends. They're like family. Your ex-lady, my ex –

COLIN   Family. That's bull ...

ESME   Barb was like a sister to me –

COLIN   She was just a friend. You wiped her out after she married Jack.

ESME   I love them. Both of them –

COLIN   Start living in the real world Es –

ESME   I want a family.

COLIN   We don't have a family yet.

ESME   I need –

COLIN   You don't.

ESME   I want –

COLIN   *I* don't!

ESME   I want a *family*!

COLIN   Well I don't. I don't!

ESME   [*Making cross on stomach.*] Cancel! Cancel! Cancel!

COLIN   [*Jumping up.*] If you dare to lay a finger on him ... [*They stare at each other.*] Oh Es ... why do you keep putting me in the adversary role?

ESME   Can you imagine Col? Can you imagine how it'll be in three years' time?

[*She looks across at the jail which begins to take shape in her mind.* COLIN *continues to drink coffee and eat dessert, unaware of the scene that is being played out as* ESME *constructs it.*]

Scene Three

P.W.P. A jail. COLIN 2 *sits, head in hands.* CRAIG *enters with two cups. He puts them on a side table. Takes one, puts his feet on the table casually.* CRAIG *should be downstage, in a small office which overlooks* COLIN 2'*s upstage cell.*

COLIN 2 [*Having watched* CRAIG *enter and settle himself.*] Well? [CRAIG *drinks.*] Are you expecting a guest? [CRAIG *doesn't reply.*] Cigarette? [*Pause.*] D'you have a cigarette? [CRAIG *doesn't reply.*] I don't smoke either. Battle situation. I'm used to it. I'm used to it you know. [*Long pause.*] How old are you? [CRAIG *doesn't reply.*] You look about six.

CRAIG I'm nearly 20! [COLIN 2] laughs. {CRAIG *jams pen into shirt pocket.*]

COLIN 2 What's your name? [CRAIG *rolls down his shirt sleeves.*] Going somewhere? I said going somewhere big shot? [*Pause.*] You and your type! [*Shakes his head.*] It's the same all over the world. Doesn't matter where you start out you end up the same. Twenty. I have a son you know – Matthew. [CRAIG *looks in mirror. Slicks his hair back.*] Lived in this mousehole all your life? [*Beat.*] I could stop anyone on the street and they'd know your name as well as they know the name of this town! [*Beat.* CRAIG *picks up his hat.*] Come over here and talk to me. I'll be out of here in half an hour. [CRAIG, *ignoring him, tries hat at different angles.*] I'll bet I've met your mother – your father was on the winning tug-of-war team at the carnival this year. We headlined it. [*Pause.*] Look lad. Give me that coffee. [CRAIG *picks up coffee and empties it into waste bin. Sits, feet on table. Drinks his own coffee.*] So this is war eh? [CRAIG *doesn't move.*] Listen –

I know more about wars than you know about ... about
... listen – listen. [*Puts head in hands.*] You think I'm mad
don't you? [*Looks up.*] I've spent half my life recording
history. Is that mad? I was once holed up in a bunker in
the Sudan – know where that is? Little backwater a few
thousand miles from this one. We were under fire from
a handful of rebels – in the mountains – I'd been taking
pictures of four tribesmen ... they came to me during a
lull in the firing. One of them had blue hives on his
tongue ... they thought I could cure ... I gave him an
aspirin. They had a camel and some corn. Yes, I
remember that – corn. Don't know where they came by
it out there ... worth more than the camel ... anyway we
were all ambushed. Before the aspirin could take effect.
The bullets that were meant for me ricocheted off the
ribs of the goddamned camel. It went down – fell on me,
I could feel its bones giving way under it, like when you
slide up the legs on a tripod. Don't know what
happened to the corn. Anyway, somehow, somehow – I
found myself in a makeshift bunker. Just me and this
kid. Like you. Just a kid. Dark eyes. At first I thought he
was caught in the crossfire too. Then I saw he was
turning a gun on me ... had a gun pointing at my
kidneys. And his hand shaking every time a shell went
off. Shaking. And I asked him for a cigarette ... [*Mimes
motion of asking when not knowing the language. Pause.*]
And he gave me one. [*Pause.*] I was on his side. I had no
way of letting him know. He thought I was the enemy. I
don't know why he didn't just ... Something distracted
him. I got away. When I got home I did a complete
analysis of the current crisis. [*Pause.*] Facts. I was
quoted in the U.S. Senate as a reliable witness. I left one
thing out. In order to get that story – I shot him.

CRAIG [*Jerks his head up.*] I don't watch.

COLIN 2 I shot him. [*Beat.*] What? What don't you watch?

CRAIG The news.

COLIN 2 You don't watch the news.

CRAIG It's always the same. [*Takes newspaper out of desk.*]

COLIN 2 Let me see that! [CRAIG *opens up comic section.*] Let me
see ... is there anything there about me? I edit that paper

goddammit! I wanna know if I made my own front page!
Is that asking too much? That's mine! [CRAIG *throws
paper in waste bin.*]
BLACKOUT

Scene Four

Some days later. ESME *sits, staring at typewriter. Sound
of typewriter offstage. The doll is propped up nearby.*

ESME Colin – [*Typing continues.*] Colin, where are you? Colin?
[*Pause.*]

COLIN [*Off. Over typing.*] Up a tree.

ESME I've been asking you to mow the lawn for weeks. [*Pause.*]
Are you in the den? [*Typing stops,* COLIN *comes and
stands in doorway looking at* ESME.] Did I interrupt you?

COLIN Look – why don't you go to bed. Write up there – any
other time you're complaining that there's no time. The
doctor said rest.

ESME I can't write. I haven't been able to write since ... [*Feels
her stomach.*] I've only written one scene and it was set
in a jail.

COLIN Well, try something new.

ESME What?

COLIN I don't know. [*Wanders out of room. Sound of typing
resumes.*]

ESME Colin.

COLIN [*Off.*] Go upstairs.

ESME On my own? What are you doing?

COLIN [*Off.*] I just have to finish this story then ... then I'll mow
the lawn.

ESME Where are you?

COLIN [*Off.*] I'm in the den.

ESME He's in the den. Colin ... I can't seem to control it. I want
to write a scene set on the patio –

COLIN [*Off.*] Go out there then –

ESME You go out there – [*Pause. Types ferociously.*] When I am
old and grey and full of fears ... [*Looks across to patio
where the next scene of P.W.P. begins as* ESME *writes it.*]

Scene Five

P.W.P. The patio. Lights dim. BARBARA, CRAIG *and* JACK
*appear in a cluster, they might sway slightly, a single unit,
phantom-like.* ESME *watches, fascinated. Turns back to
typewriter; as she does so they stop moving. She
continues to type. Lights remain on her, fade on* BARBARA,
CRAIG *and* JACK.

*Lights up on patio. Hammock which was formerly
empty is now bulging.* JACK *roams the patio. He is
wearing soiled rugby clothes, the same as* COLIN *wore in
previous scene. He has a camera. Begins to photograph
the doll, whose head can be seen poking out over the
hammock.*

JACK [*To doll.*] Smile. Click. Don't be coy dear, I know those
teeth aren't real. Smile, and again, now – present arms.
[*The doll's arms go up.*] Eyes right, yes, sexy. [*Doll's head
moves.*] How about a nice goose step for Uncle Jack ...
[*The leg appears.*] Goosy goosy gander ... clickety click ...
here, I bought you a present ... [*Gives doll a toy gun.*]
Don't tell your mother. You've got a good leg, have you
got another? [*Two doll's legs appear.*] Ah, so, shall we
dance? [ESME 2 *sticks her leg up over the hammock.*
JACK, *still dangling the doll, examines* ESME 2's *ankle.*]
Swollen. [*Peers down into hammock.*] Acutely swollen.
[*Dances with doll.*] Oh how we danced on the night we
were wed. [*Thrusts doll away from him.*] Did you just
piss? [*Whispers.*] Well, she won't have to wash nappies
this time around, they're all paper now – hope she'll do
better with this one. Colin aways wanted a nice doll for
his birthday. [*Dangles doll. Sings.*] Little Shirley Temple,
she bought a penny doll. She washed it, she dressed it.
Then she let it fall. [*Drops doll. Walks out laughing.*]

ESME [*At typewriter.*] She's just for practice, you're in a
liberated house Jack. We've planned this child. We're
going to give it the best. A happy life – a non-sexist
education. We're going to take such care of this child ...

160

Scene Five

[*During this last line* CRAIG *has come on, he stands behind the hammock, cradling the doll, smiling at her, mocking.* ESME *yells, frantic, as* CRAIG *leaves.*] Colin – Col – where are you?

COLIN 2 [*Enters, brings on barbecue with corn.* JACK *joins him at patio table.* COLIN *holds up glass as he did in Scene II.*] Esme doesn't drink wine.

JACK Esme's getting boring in her old age. [ESME, *at typewriter, shakes her head.*] The lads know you're in town.

COLIN 2 Have you played yet?

JACK Not yet. [*Sniffs himself.*] They're waiting for you.

ESME [*Addressing the typewriters.*] He's not playing rugby, he's only just come home!

COLIN 2 [*Talking over* ESME.] I don't know if I can get away –

JACK You'd better be there that's all. My boy's playing his first game with us today.

COLIN 2 Craig? [ESME *shows signs of agitation.*]

JACK Non-sexist education! My father never came near me till I was old enough to wear his soccer boots and lift a pint mug. [*Pushes doll with his foot.*] I'm none the worse for it. I never saw a bloody rugby ball till I came over here ... never ate paté on the patio and drank fancy wine. Still don't. [*Leans forward confidingly.*] No one expected me to be some kind of male penguin and sit on the egg for six months while the female of the species cooked paté. [*Leaning back.*] And my son's none the worse for it. He was up every morning delivering papers when he was ten years old ...

[*During this speech* CRAIG *comes and stands behind* JACK. COLIN 2 *does not see him. The men leave the table,* CRAIG *remains, seats himself.* BARBARA *joins him. (These changes should be slow, almost dreamlike; no one pays any attention to the bulging hammock.)* ESME *puts her head on the typewriter, finally looks over at* BARBARA *and* CRAIG, *and they begin to speak.*]

BARBARA You're going to be nice to her. You hear me?

CRAIG She's not my mother. You are.

BARBARA It doesn't matter what she did. [*She gets up.*]

CRAIG Barbara – I don't want to –

161

BARBARA We're proud of you, your father and I. Never forget that. You're a real man!
[*Lights down on* BARBARA *and* CRAIG *and up on* ESME *who rises from typewriter.* COLIN 2 *and* JACK *resume their places at the table.* CRAIG *and* BARBARA *exit.*]

COLIN 2 [*Offers* JACK *a head of corn from barbeque.* JACK *pushes it away.*] When I'm away I – I freeze. And when I'm back here – nothing. Not for her, not for the Bump ... I don't feel.

JACK Few of us can afford the luxury.

COLIN 2 I once killed someone Jack. [*Pause.*] It was him or me.

JACK On the job? [COLIN 2 *nods.*] I'm sure you made the right choice. [COLIN 2 *stares ahead bleakly.* JACK *puts his arm round his shoulders, old pal style.*] We've all been there.

COLIN 2 Don't tell Esme.

JACK She probably knows. [COLIN 2 *shakes his head.* JACK *reassures him. The bulge in the hammock moves.*]

COLIN 2 You know what I like about you Jack? I can talk to you. It's ... [*Trails off.*]

JACK It's the job isn't it? It's no job for a man with a family, right? Since when have you thought of yourself as a married man? That's why it's lasted this long.

COLIN 2 It was somebody's son.

JACK We all are.

COLIN 2 [*Gets up.*] I'm gonna change for the game. Give me five minutes, okay?
[*Lights fade on* JACK, *alone at table, laughing.* ESME *exits leaving him onstage. Slow fade to black.*]

Scene Six

Full light. A prenatal class in a bare room. We watch COLIN *and* ESME *for a while. They are lying on the floor a few yards apart.* PADDY *enters.*

PADDY Good. Good. Now deeper. Breathe deeply. Deeper. Good girl. I can give you 15 minutes – good – [*They both follow her instructions silently for a few seconds.*] Esme?

ESME Whoops. Fell asleep.

PADDY Colin's doing better than you are.

COLIN Piece of cake. [*Exchanges conspiratorial glance with* PADDY, *as* PADDY *takes* ESME's *necklace off.*]

ESME [*To* PADDY.] I was dreaming of you. You remind me of someone. Who does she remind you of Colin?

COLIN No one in particular.

ESME She does me.

PADDY All right, let's start again. [COLIN *hasn't stopped.*] I want you to count to five, very slowly ... Inhale, exhale ...

COLIN One, two, three, four, five ...

ESME We're high-risk parents. It's not just me. The sperm loses its pizzazz after the prime years. Isn't that so? How old is a man when he's in his prime? He peaks ten years before a woman even if he does play rugby. Isn't that so?

PADDY Esme.

ESME Well, you're the expert.

PADDY There is no reason to suppose that yours will be anything other than a normal pregnancy provided you follow –

ESME Listen Paddy, I don't think I can ... go through with this. [COLIN *signals* PADDY *not to be concerned.*]

PADDY Lie back and relax. Everyone's nervous the first time.

ESME It's not my first time.

PADDY Our bodies forget.

ESME Our bodies forget.

PADDY [*Soothing.*] So let's remind them.

ESME It doesn't want to remember.

COLIN Es ...!

ESME [*Sits up.*] Look – lines. [*She points to her face.*] Gaps. [*She points to her teeth.* PADDY *lays her down.*] You know how some cats don't care for their kittens?

PADDY That's not going to happen.

ESME And some cats eat them.

COLIN Cool it Es.

PADDY Relax. Look how well Colin's doing.

ESME Rotten Tom!

COLIN Every sperm a bullseye! [ESME *yowls.*] See how they spray! [*Makes ack-ack of machine gun, sits up, sprays her with bullets.* PADDY *is disconcerted by this. They lapse into silence. Lie back. Breathe.*]

ESME Does your husband tell you what's on his mind?

PADDY My husband's very supportive. Like yours.

ESME I'm being a nuisance. [*Relaxes.*] It's good of you to see us on our own. I suppose I was disruptive in the class. I often am ... they throw me out of rehearsals. I have a right to stay ... but they throw me out.

PADDY [*Adjusting* COLIN'*s position.*] Better. You're getting the hang of it. [*Beat.*]

COLIN There've been studies that show that when a person imagines running, small but measurable amounts of contractions actually take place in the muscles associated with running.

ESME Imagine that!

COLIN The same neurological pathways are excited by imagined running as by actual running.

ESME Imagine running.

COLIN Physiologically.

ESME Listen to the wheels squeak on the chariot of fire!

PADDY It's true. We can be in sympathy with each other.

ESME Words!

PADDY He can help ...

ESME He has all the words.

PADDY He can help if you'd only ...

ESME Words.

COLIN Shut up! I want to do this.

ESME Words. But where are the feelings? How does this feel Bump? [*Makes a bongo out of her stomach.* COLIN *reaches across instinctively to stop her.* PADDY *calms her. She relaxes and breathes deeply.*] When we are old and grey and full of fears –

COLIN Tears.

ESME Fears.

COLIN Full of tears – [*Calm, they breathe deeply.*]

COLIN Tears.

ESME Fears.

COLIN Tears.

ESME Schmears!

Scene Six

[*Silence.*]

PADDY Are you ready? [ESME *nods.*] Now I want you to try panting. Colin, reach over and pinch. [COLIN *reaches and pinches* ESME's *thigh.*] That's right.

ESME Harder. [COLIN *obeys.*] Make it hurt.

PADDY You've prepared your song?

ESME Forty seconds one contraction right? [*To* COLIN.] Time it – ah – ah [*He is about to stop pinching in order to look at his watch. Sings fast.*]

> I love to go a-wandering
> Along a mountain track
> And as I go I love to sing
> My knapsack on my back.
> Valderee ...

[*Nudges* COLIN.]

COLIN [*Obediently.*] Valderee.

ESME Valderaa ...

COLIN Valderaa ...

ESME Valderee ...

COLIN Valderee ...

PADDY Push.

ESME Valderahahahahahaha [*To* COLIN.] Harder – hurt me! haaa! [*Yells.*]

PADDY Push! – Colin, stay with it, harder – the final contractions are enough to blast you right across this room! Harder! [COLIN *sits up, then gets to his feet.*]

ESME [*Continues to sing.*] I wave my hat to all I see, and they wave back to me, and blackbirds call ...

COLIN See you in a few minutes ... [*To* PADDY.] Need a smoke. [*Exits. He can be seen pacing on the periphery of the scene.*]

PADDY Try it at home.

ESME [*Sits up and stares after him.*] He doesn't smoke. [*Beat.*] I pushed too hard. [*Beat.*] I love him you know. You mustn't think ... we've been together a long time. I thought we ... knew each other.

PADDY You do.

ESME What do you know?

PADDY I sense it. An understanding.

165

ESME   War games. We play war games. It helps keep the balance of power. [PADDY *laughs*.] So you'd say they were necessary.

PADDY   For some.

ESME   Openness. That's necessary?

PADDY   Yes.

ESME   Well, he's not open.

PADDY   Hm.

ESME   Either he doesn't have any goddamned feelings or he hides them so well that ... we used to be equals.

PADDY   Sssh!

ESME   He killed a young boy. What do you think of that?

PADDY   Don't be silly.

ESME   You know how I found out? [*Silence.*] I read about it in the newspaper. His paper. He didn't tell me. Well? [*Silence.*] So what do you think of him now?

PADDY   I'm sure there's an explanation.

ESME   Oh sure there's an explanation. It's all in there, in the paper. He was ambushed in the Sudan – he hid behind a camel.

PADDY   [*Laughs.*] Oh, you mean it wasn't in Canada?

ESME   What?

PADDY   Well – in some countries life's less important – [ESME *sits back, silenced.*] I don't think life's not important –

ESME   He killed a child for a piece of news.

PADDY   I mean life itself – of course that's ...

ESME   That's worse than anything I've ever done. He confessed but not to me. The irony is that I have to be pregnant with his child in order to have time to sit around reading newspapers. I'm usually too busy. [*Beat.*] Is it true that if you kill once it's easier the next time?

PADDY   I don't know. Ask him.

ESME   We have a pact. We never talk to each other about anything connected with our work. It's what's kept us together. [*Beat.*]

PADDY   It was probably self-defence.

ESME   He's a war correspondent. He feeds on war. I always tried to tempt his appetite. Now I don't know how to stop.

PADDY   Maybe you're making too much of it.

ESME It used to be they thought war was what a man had to do. Now ... [*Shrugs.*] Well, what does a man have to do? [*Beat.*] Maybe we don't need them – there's a thought. We don't need heroes any more, that's for sure. I don't want that for my child – do you?

PADDY Society's changing.

ESME I've changed. I wanted to try again before it was too late. [*Beat.*] I wasn't unkind to the first one – I just ... I kind of abandoned him – I wonder now if I was sick – I remember feeling so claustrophobic and he was always crying – my friend Barbara had to come in and ...

PADDY And now you feel guilty.

ESME Now? Always. Always ... [*Beat.*]

PADDY [*Comforting.*] Esme ...

ESME I've been wondering if I can take this on alone.

PADDY You'll see things differently when ...

ESME [*Pulling back.*] See, I'm living with a man who kills. You know something Paddy? I don't even think I like men. They're alien beings ... I always thought of him as my best friend, and now he feels like the enemy ...

PADDY He's a very nice man – you should see some who come through here!

ESME I'm driving him away. [*Beat.*] What if it's another boy? It might happen ... Oh God, what am I saying. What am I doing? He has to help me through this – he can't leave me ... he can't go back to his wars ... how could he ... how could he do that? And not tell me! How many times?

PADDY [*Kneeling beside her.*] It'll be all right. It'll be all right. [*Strokes her hair.*]

ESME It will?

PADDY Of course.

ESME I want this baby you know. More than anything. I didn't last time.

PADDY I know.

ESME I'm so scared.

PADDY I know.

ESME They're going to interview us on TV. Parenting over 40. Half the people out there don't even have sex after they're 40. [*Beat.*] He wants a boy.

PADDY Just relax for a while. That's it. Relax.

167

ESME You know what I'm looking forward to most?

PADDY What?

ESME Being able to lie flat on my stomach again. [PADDY *laughs.* ESME *lying on the ground, takes up her necklace, holds it over her stomach, making it swing in circles. Looks up at* PADDY.] You remind me of someone Paddy. [PADDY *settles and soothes her, then exits to discover* COLIN. *Light holds on* ESME *during the rest of the scene, dimming slowly.*]

PADDY [*Seeing* COLIN *who's standing outside her office.*] Oh?

COLIN I wanted to ask you ... you've been talking to her. [PADDY *nods.*] She's left alone more than she should be –

PADDY You're a newsman. Must be an exciting life.

COLIN It's not particularly glamorous if that's what she's telling you.

PADDY Must be dangerous.

COLIN Not really. [*Beat.*] So how was I doing?

PADDY You were doing fine. [*Beat.*]

COLIN I just wanted to ...

PADDY Why don't you sit down?

COLIN I wanted to talk to an expert.

PADDY I'm only a nurse Colin.

COLIN I know. But - you're seeing women every day. Pregnant. [*Beat.*] Does it make a difference when they're over 40? I mean I've read about it but ...

PADDY She's had all the tests –

COLIN I mean ... is it likely to unbalance her?

PADDY Unbalance?

COLIN Well – I mean, what's going on with her?

PADDY I get the feeling you two should talk more.

COLIN We talk all the time.

PADDY Real talk.

COLIN I mean all I want to know is if it's normal – the way she goes on? Considering she is left alone a lot –

PADDY Everyone reacts differently.

COLIN I try – you've seen me try.

PADDY Well – at least you know it's for a limited period.

COLIN But after?

PADDY Bliss. [*She smiles.*]

Scene Six

COLIN Twenty years of bliss? [*Pause.* ESME *is seen to be listening.*]

PADDY This is the first time for you?

COLIN The first that I know of –

PADDY And you're scared.

COLIN No. I just had some questions. I don't want advice.

PADDY Go ahead.

COLIN Well ... [*He trails off. Silence.*]

PADDY Look – if you'd like me to recommend some books.

COLIN We've read all the books.

PADDY Then what's bothering you?

COLIN Just now – was she talking about Craig? She had another child you know. She wasn't good at it. Parenting – that's what it's called these days isn't it? Parenting. She wasn't good at –

PADDY I'm not a psychiatrist – I can tell you what's going on in her body, but –

COLIN All right then, tell me that.

PADDY There are certain hormonal changes taking place.

COLIN That's all?

PADDY She may seem obsessive.

COLIN Well what about me? Are there hormonal changes in men? Is it true that a man can breast feed if ...

PADDY I think there have been cases, I haven't studied the literature.

COLIN I feel like – I'm acting strange – I mean look at me – even being here, what good's it gonna do? Valderee. Is this going to go on – after it's born? I mean ... I'm too old to be asking these questions right? Sex for instance.

PADDY Pardon?

COLIN That can continue of course, when she's feeding it. But will she want ...?

PADDY Nothing needs to stop.

COLIN That's what it says in the books. [*Pause.*] The parks are filled with grey-haired men pushing bugs.

PADDY Buggies?

COLIN [*Nods.*] But they're on their second time around. They've married their secretaries or their students. Their wives are young. Resilient. [*Pause.*] I find myself looking at their young wives. Is that natural? I never did it before. I always looked down on the guys who did. [*Pause.*] She wasn't good to the last one – said she was too young; when it was three she ran off with another man. We've had a perfectly happy marriage for 15 years. We've trusted each other, we've never been proprietory – given each other all the space. Listen, how many couples do you know who've been married for 15 years and ... Don't tell her, I mean – we discussed it all. I just didn't anticipate that she'd ... change.

PADDY Colin. I have to get back to her. [*Shuffles through some papers.*] Why don't you tell her what you've just told me?

COLIN [*Shakes his head.*] You haven't understood.

PADDY Then why don't you try group therapy? [*Smiles. Exits. COLIN remains, plainly horrified at the prospect.*] BLACKOUT

Scene Seven

Evening. Three weeks later. An auditorium. ESME *is stacking chairs. She tries one on another, then reverses them. Her heart is not in the task.* COLIN *enters and stands behind her. She jumps. He has a bag, a camera, a briefcase.*

ESME You were out there then? [*Indicates auditorium.* COLIN *nods.*] I didn't notice you in the ...

COLIN I was at the back. Here – [*Takes chairs and stacks them.*]

ESME I can do it. [*Pause.*] When'd you get back?

COLIN Landed at seven.

ESME Seven? [COLIN *nods.*] Our guests haven't shown yet. They called yesterday from North Carolina. [*Pause.*] So? [*Pause.*]

COLIN I missed the first half.

ESME It was a benefit. For Amnesty.

COLIN I saw the flier.

ESME Everyone's going for a beer at Maxine's. Shall we? [COLIN *sits on a chair,* ESME *sits on another.*] So ... good trip?

170

COLIN Usual.

ESME We missed you. Me and the Bump.

COLIN How's he doing?

ESME I think he's going to miss his deadline. [*Pause.*] So –
what did you make of it?

COLIN What?

ESME The reading, of course. The goddamn reading – since
you were here for it.

COLIN You knew I'd be here.

ESME I knew you'd rush here straight from the airport?

COLIN Yes.

ESME And? [*Pause.*]

COLIN When I left I was married to a playwright.

ESME The theatre's dead.

COLIN That was sudden.

ESME It's elitist. I want to get my message across to the rag-
readers and the box-watchers. Like you do. [COLIN
shakes his head.] You know what theatre's best for?
Showing pain. But nobody wants to pay to see pain: not
when they see it written all over the breakfast table
every morning.

COLIN So you're going to spend your time performing for
Amnesty.

ESME I've got things I have to say. [*Pause.*] Doubleday's
bringing the poems out in rush edition. They've asked
me to do a reading in New York.

COLIN *Poems?*

ESME Look, it was nothing personal. I should just finish
stacking these ... chairs.

COLIN Sit down Esme. [ESME *sits.*] *Media Mumbles* – is that
what you called them?

ESME Did you recognize that piece before I said it was yours?

COLIN *Media Mumbles.*

ESME Good name eh? They liked the bit about the camel – the
way its legs folded. Hey – listen, here's one I didn't use –
the committee didn't think it fitted the theme. All the
readings had to be about torture – it's from *Maclean's* – I
didn't change a word – just as she was writ in the good
ol' media – [*Reads.*]
Singing star triumphs.

171

On tour recently to promote
her recent record,
the Tennessee dirt farmer's daughter
with
the super teased hairdo
and
the remarkable figure,
needled her audience
about
her
high profile.
'I see a lot of you brought your binoculars ...
I know why. You don't fool me.
You wanted to see
if
these wigs
was as big
as
you thought they was.'
Isn't that torture? – or this one ... [COLIN *gestures that
he's heard enough.*] So you see, you're not the only one
who strings his words together like a third grader.
[COLIN *picks up a chair and places it loudly, squarely on
the ground.*] Unfair. Since I've been reading the papers
I've been looking carefully at your stuff – it's way ahead
of the rest. Stands out. Cross my heart.

COLIN   You try writing decent prose after you've just ploughed
your way through a goddamned charnel house. What
do you expect me to do?

ESME   I expect you to tell the truth.

COLIN   I tell the truth.

ESME   You tell your edited version. A newspaperman's version.

COLIN   That's what I am. You don't want me to be what I am?

ESME   I want you to stop pretending to be a hero.

COLIN   When do I ever say I'm a hero?

ESME   You maintain a heroic silence. [*Pause.*] Look at you now.
You jerk off across the front page of tomorrow's fire-
lighter, yet when you're with me you keep your zipper
done up so tight you ...

COLIN The other guys – the other guys' wives have some sense of what they go through. [*Pause.*] All right then, all right – I'll talk ... I'll come home and I'll spill it all into your lap.

ESME No. No – you're not listening.

COLIN Listening happens to be my job. You know what I hear? I hear a honky screaming out my most – my most intimate moments in the most public arena she can find. You're cruel Esme.

ESME I'm not cruel!

COLIN Maybe you don't even know what you're doing – that scares the shit out of me –

ESME I know what I'm doing!

COLIN Well, you don't know what you want!

ESME I want you to stay home, that's what I want. I want our child to live with an ordinary nine-to-five father who doesn't play with guns – and if I have to shout to make you hear –

COLIN Ordinary? Since when have you been attracted to the ordinary?

ESME Since you got me pregnant.

COLIN And you had nothing to do with it? Are you willing to stop banging on the typewriter and be an ordinary mother?

ESME I already have. All I've written is two lousy scenes.

COLIN Oh? Ordinary women produce *Media Mumbles* do they?

ESME One in a prison and one ...

COLIN How do you think our kid's gonna enjoy coming home ... coming home and finding his old man held up for ridicule in front of a gaggle of ...

ESME I haven't held you up. It was the media. I was ... holding up the media.

COLIN Held up ...

ESME Holed up. Bunkered.

COLIN By a bunch of bleached women!

ESME This is a hold-up. [*Points imaginary gun. They face each other, furious.* ESME *gives way first.*] They aren't bleached ...

COLIN Bleached middle-class women.

173

ESME   They aren't middle-class. All right – all right your piece won't be included in the book. I was wrong.

COLIN   You were more than just wrong – what do you think I do when I'm away?

ESME   Why do you always have to diminish what I do?

COLIN   You don't have the first notion of what you do. Of what you just did! That article was ... one of the – the ... most painful things I ever wrote.

ESME   And you didn't show it to me. You didn't tell me. [*Pause.*] So why don't we both give up?

COLIN   I am never giving up – while there's a job to be done and I can still do it – I'll be there. I'll be there because I'm better than all the rest –

ESME   And so was I.

COLIN   Then go to it!

ESME   You can bring me a souvenir back from your next trip, to prove what you do. A pinkie or a big toe. How about an ashtray with 'present from Santiago' on the rim, and a few ashes in it. Human ashes. [COLIN *picks up chair, hurls it at her. Misses.*] You could've ... hurt the baby. [COLIN *rights the chair, sits on it, trembling.*] Well, how do I know it wasn't just a story? That's what it was, wasn't it? Col? You'd've told me if you'd actually – God – I'll bet it's not the first time! I'll bet ...

COLIN   Are you through?

ESME   You're so goddamned stoical.

COLIN   I said are you ...?

ESME   And I said did you shoot? [*Silence.*]

COLIN   Did you have a coat?

ESME   Well? [COLIN *puts his coat on.*] Bloody hero.

COLIN   It's just a job, Esme.

ESME   Just a job?

COLIN   I've kept my mouth shut because you never wanted into my professional life and I never wanted into yours.

ESME   You hate the theatre.

COLIN   And you hate the real world.

ESME   That's unfair! ...

COLIN   I come back from a bad stint, it's like – it's like ... it takes me a few days to even believe in this place ... the trivia

174

... people acting plays ... people giving poetry readings ...
all the well-meaning people ... [ESME *gets her coat,
cradles her stomach.*] To believe that nothing's going on
under the surface – that there isn't a jail full of poor
s.o.b.'s screaming day and night while somebody pulls
the flesh off strip by strip. At first I find myself confused
... it takes a while to unwind and realize ...

ESME   What a bland lot we are. [*Long pause.*]

COLIN   You should just thank God that our son's being born
into a healthy environment.

ESME   What's healthy about it? Oh Col – [*Stretches out hand,
he pulls away.*]

COLIN   As a matter of fact I did bring you a souvenir.

ESME   Oh?

COLIN   Tree bark.

ESME   Tree bark?

COLIN   They diaper their children with it. [*Brings out package.*]

ESME   Who?

COLIN   They chew it first. [*Gives it to her. ESME drops the
present. Looks around, picks up her manuscript, takes
the page she has just read from, and chews on it.*] There
are babies being born every second of every day out
there. [ESME *chews.*] People die every day. Real death.
No bags of red dye under their shirts. If they own shirts.

ESME   So what does it feel like to kill?

COLIN   You've done your share. [ESME *stares at him, suddenly
breaks. Sobs.* COLIN *approaches her, puts his arm
around her. She almost chokes. He cups his hand under
her chin as if she were a child. Obediently she spits the
chewed paper into his hand. Laughing.*] Good job there
isn't an audience.

ESME   I want you to stay home. I want you to stay home with
us. We'll make it together.

COLIN   I'll see what I can do.

ESME   Maybe we could go out west. After the baby's born ...
you could get a job easily.

COLIN   I'm arranging more home leaves.

ESME   Well, Jack and Barb did it. We'll ask them to help. Jack
can get you a job ...

COLIN [*Freezes. Looks around for a way out. Spots tape recorder.*] Is that thing on?

ESME For the reading. [COLIN *yanks the cord out.*] For the reading, that's all.

COLIN Jesus Esme. Jesus!

ESME For the reading.

COLIN You use me up. Every bit of me. You just pick me dry. [*Picks up his briefcase and camera.*]

ESME Where are you going?

COLIN To eat. Bland food, in some bland bar; maybe the bland barman'll tell me something I don't already know about all the bland people who do benefits for Amnesty.

ESME Col ...

COLIN Go home. Go home and rest ... and read Dr. Spock. [COLIN *exits.*]

ESME Colin! Don't blow it Esme. Don't blow it. [*Goes to tape recorder, turns switch and watches tape rewind. Slow fade to dim light.* JACK *and* BARB *appear on periphery and remain there.*]

Scene Eight

P.W.P. COLIN 2 *and* CRAIG: *the jail.* CRAIG *is drinking beer.*

COLIN 2 Do you know what a playwright is? [*Pause.*] Someone who plays – is that what you think?

CRAIG Someone who plays.

COLIN 2 No – you don't know. Why would you? She hasn't written anything ... not since ... She wasn't that well known anyway. Her stuff's too complex. Like her.

CRAIG Why don't you just go play with yourself?

COLIN 2 What?

CRAIG Quit.

COLIN 2 Quit?

CRAIG I don't want to have nothing to do with you okay?

COLIN 2 Well you're going to.

CRAIG Enough!

COLIN 2 You're in charge?

CRAIG I said that's enough.

COLIN 2 What's your name?

CRAIG Listen ...

COLIN 2 Name!

CRAIG I said ...

COLIN 2 Boss. Is that your name?

CRAIG I said ...

COLIN 2 Boss.

CRAIG Now look ...

COLIN 2 What do you know about women, Boss?

CRAIG I don't wanna hear no more. You just go on and on.

COLIN 2 Don't keep staring at me, Boss.

CRAIG Shit!

COLIN 2 I'll turn you round to face the wall. D'you have brown paper pasted on behind? [CRAIG *paces, not knowing what to do, not listening.*] She won this round. She won. She won every round even when she seemed to be losing. She put me in here, d'you know that? I tied myself to a desk for her. I tried to change for her. Talking to each other. There's no real contact. Nothing. Nothing. Come over here what'syourname. Is that a gun you're wearing? Come here I said. Goddammit don't they teach you to obey in this outfit? How come they've left you in charge anyway? How old did you say you are? When they find out who I am I'll be out of here so fast ... as soon as they know who ... I was. [CRAIG *makes a whimpering sound. Clenches fists.*] You think you're in love – you try to narrow it down, you pin everything on one person – you put four walls around it. It's a fantasy ... you can't contain it. It's a fantasy, we're always trying to contain ... look for limits. Without limits we go mad, don't we? [CRAIG *leaves the office and goes into the cell.*]

CRAIG [*Indicating* COLIN's *jacket.*] Take that off!

COLIN 2 We go mad.

CRAIG Take it off.

COLIN 2 The dumbest thing of all is trying to get it down in newsprint. That's what we'll end up, as you know. Newsprint. Thinking you know whose side you're on ... risking your life to chase ambulances. Her stuff fed on it.

177

CRAIG Take that off.

COLIN 2 Is that a gun?

CRAIG Take ...

COLIN 2 Look whatsyourname you ...

CRAIG Now.

COLIN 2 Over there they give kids guns to play with. They tell them it's a game, but it's not a game – it's war. Right? Right. Boss. [CRAIG *tears* COLIN's *jacket off and sticks his gun in* COLIN's *ribs.* COLIN *slowly begins to unbutton his shirt. Slow fade out.*]

Scene Nine

ESME *and* COLIN's *house. Later.* ESME *is reading Dr. Spock. She has a drink. Leans across and turns on tape recorder. We hear a recording of the final part of scene seven (the part of the scene before* COLIN *discovers the tape recorder).* ESME *turns it down. Reads aloud, over recording.*

ESME A baby starts by using its head. It's a gradual process by which a baby learns to control his body. It starts with the head and gradually works down to the hands, trunk and legs.
[ESME 2 *walks on, arranges a copy of Dr. Spock on a lectern.* ESME *looks at kitchen window. A slide is projected which reads 'Poet Gives Last Public Reading.'*]

ESME 2 Just as soon as he's born
He knows how to suck.
And if something touches
his cheek – the nipple
or your finger for example
he tries to reach it with his mouth.
If you try
to hold
his head
still
he becomes angry right away

178

and twists to get it
free.
Probably
he has this instinct
to keep
from getting smothered.
Parents ask –
when does he learn to see?
This is a gradual process
like everything else.
Provided you don't poke his little eyes out!
[ESME *crosses to typewriter, taking tape recorder and
books with her.* ESME 2 *crosses to kitchen table and
continues to read Dr. Spock as* ESME *was doing.*]

Scene Ten

P.W.P. Lights up on BARB *and* COLIN 2 *sitting formally on
the couch. The start of the scene has a hesitant quality as
it forms in* ESME's *imagination.*

COLIN 2   I thought you'd still be in bare feet and bangles, Barbara.
BARBARA   That's history.
COLIN 2   I'm glad. Nice little place. Is that a peacock on the rail?
[*Looks outside.* BARBARA *nods.*] And mountains ... think
I'll fit in here? The interview went well. I think they'll
hire me. [*Pause.*]
BARBARA   Yes of course, if you'd ...
COLIN 2   I don't want advice.
BARBARA   I'm taking a real estate course.
COLIN 2   Real estate? You? [*Laughs.*] Does Esme know?
BARBARA   She just found out. [*Beat.*] She's jealous.
COLIN 2   Of real estate?
ESME   [*At typewriter.*] No. No not that. Try this –
[ESME 2 *does not look up. Shift in mood here as* ESME
decides what she is doing with this scene. BARB *and*
COLIN *become more intimate.*]
BARBARA   No. No not of real estate.

179

COLIN 2 She's never jealous. [*Pause.*] You're still attractive.

BARBARA Surprised?

COLIN 2 I'd forgotten

BARBARA She'll be jealous.

COLIN 2 We're not proprietary with each other.

BARBARA But she's jealous. I know.

COLIN 2 How?

BARBARA Because she's my sister. She'll find out you were here last night when she comes out here.

COLIN 2 Are we going to make a habit of this? [BARB *puts her hand on his knee.*] I'm not sure that we should. [*Pause.*] It'll be a help to her having you here. Since she had the baby she's agreed not to do any more public appearances.

BARBARA Es? But that's part of her life.

COLIN 2 It'll work out, you'll see. The country air'll do wonders. [*He takes her hand, then takes her in his arms.*]
BLACKOUT

Scene Eleven

Darkness. ESME and COLIN's house. We hear COLIN putting his key in the lock and coming through door.

COLIN Couldn't face Chinese again – whoops, why are you sitting in the dark?
[*Full lights up. ESME is sitting in bed.*]

ESME Just wondering how to change the scene. From the big lake to the small pond. A backdrop of mountains maybe. [*A mountain scene is projected onto kitchen window blind. Meanwhile COLIN takes his coat off and dumps a package on the table.*]

ESME Elephant Mountain. That's a good name – it's in the atlas. I'd be able to see it through my kitchen window. Every day. Every time I yawn I'll swallow it. [*Pause.*] I'm writing a play about us.

COLIN In the dark? [*Goes over and pulls window blind up.*] Let's have some real light on it. [*He stands for a moment in the projected image then it is gone.*] Fried chicken okay?

ESME [*Heaving herself off the bed.*] Big city tables and chairs would look different in small town kitchens. [*Shifting table.*] I'm going to make you the editor of a small-time newspaper out west, like Jack.

COLIN Me? Most unlikely.

ESME Jack's in it too. You see I thought I'd try to put you in my position, so you'd really know how it feels.

COLIN [*Laughs.*] Not pregnant! [*Brings supper upstairs.*]

ESME No. I'll be three years down the road. You don't really mind if I write about you do you?

COLIN If it keeps you happy. [ESME *looks at him, not understanding this geniality.*] We'll have it on our laps. [*Supper.*] Back in bed with you. Move. You're supposed to keep your feet up.

ESME I've kept my feet up for two weeks. Is there still a world out there?

COLIN Soon be D day. [*Pats her stomach. Removes doll from couch tenderly.*] There we go Liza.

ESME [*Reaches up, takes his hand.*] Love you.

COLIN [*Kisses her. Undoes package.*] It's not as hot as it was. I dropped by the office after I picked it up.

ESME You're supposed to be on leave.

COLIN Bad news I'm afraid.

ESME Bad news?

COLIN They want me out of here – day after tomorrow latest – Russ Pringle's come down with malaria.

ESME Russ Pringle's come down with malaria.

COLIN Poor s.o.b. – last year he was shot up in Guatemala, and now ...

ESME They want you to fly out.

COLIN Well, I've put it off as long as I can. Is it my fault you're late?

ESME [*Lightly.*] No. No. It's mine. So you're going?

COLIN I don't have any alternative. You think I'd miss being in on this if ... It's okay. Everything's set up. I tracked Jack down. They're heading up here right away –

ESME You spoke with Jack?

COLIN Yes. And I checked with the doctor. He knows the situation.

ESME So it's all taken care of.

COLIN As well as is humanly possible.

ESME And all I have to do is lie back and push.

COLIN Just keep your feet up like a good girl.

ESME [*Sticking foot up in air.*] Swollen. [*Beat.*] What happens if I go on pushing – I push everything out – my ribs, my lungs ... [*Pause.*] They strap you down you know –

COLIN Look Es. It's not my fault. You know if I could change it –

ESME Do you believe that having nightmares about something makes it happen?

COLIN No.

ESME That writing it down makes it happen?

COLIN No.

ESME No. It's all Russ Pringle's fault.

COLIN It's nobody's fault. The whole Mid East thing is ... [*Sighs.*]

ESME It's the Middle East's fault. Why don't they understand that when they sneeze in Beirut everyone in North America has to rush for the kleenex? Don't they consider how they disrupt people's lives? [*Beat.*]

COLIN [*Arranging paper plates.*] Calm down.

ESME Why don't they write their own history? [*Pause.*] Hold me Colin.

COLIN Let's eat first. There's still some warmth here ...

ESME Breasts and legs.

COLIN Es. I said I'm sorry. What else? [*Takes a piece of chicken on a plastic fork and tries to tempt her. She picks up french fries and throws them at him. He reciprocates and throws a handful back. They battle with the food, laughing.*]

COLIN Come on ... come on ... it's just like mother used to make.

ESME It's finger lickin' better ...

COLIN How does this sit on your stomach? [*Aims a single french fry.*]

ESME Chicken!

COLIN [*Makes chicken noises.*]

ESME [*Beside herself laughing.*] Oh Jack ...!

COLIN [*Stops suddenly.*] Jack?

ESME Oh sorry, sorry. He's on my mind that's all. [*Laughs.*] Did he tell you?

Scene Eleven

COLIN Who?

ESME Jack.

COLIN [*Stops battling.*]

ESME Well did he? Did he tell you who's with them? They're all together, travelling up the coast.

COLIN Who?

ESME Craig. Craig's coming.
[*Freeze. Lights fade on* ESME *and* COLIN.]

Scene Twelve

P.W.P. Lights up on jail as in scene seven. CRAIG *is still holding the gun.* BARBARA *and* JACK *are not present.* COLIN 2 *and* CRAIG *face each other.*

COLIN 2 So what is your goddamned name?

CRAIG MacNeil.

COLIN 2 You a Mc or a Mac?

CRAIG What?

COLIN 2 Scottish?

CRAIG Listen ...

COLIN 2 First name?

CRAIG Listen ...

COLIN 2 Listen to me boy. First name?

CRAIG That's enough.

COLIN 2 You're in charge.

CRAIG I said that's enough.

COLIN 2 Boss McNeil. Is that your name?

CRAIG Enough!

COLIN 2 Boss.

CRAIG Look ...

COLIN 2 Name! I said name!

CRAIG Craig MacNeil.

ESME [*Quietly.*] Craig.

Act II Scene One A

Bedroom. ESME *has the typewriter balanced awkwardly on the bed. Sheets of paper around her. She glances up, stares and as she does so ...*

Scene One B

P.W.P. COLIN 2 *and* ESME 2 *take their places at the kitchen table.*

There is a view of Elephant Mountain through the window of the kitchen.

The scene should mirror Act One Scene Two.

ESME 2 More ice cream?

COLIN 2 No thanks.

ESME 2 All natural ingredients. No additives. [COLIN 2 *looks at her as if additives meant poison.*] Don't wipe your mouth on that serviette.

COLIN 2 What are serviettes for?

ESME 2 Not the linen ones. I don't want to keep washing them.

COLIN 2 You should use paper ones.

ESME 2 You said you didn't like paper ones.

COLIN 2 Did I?

ESME 2 Yes. Yes you did. [*Pause.*] Isn't it true?

COLIN 2 If I said it then I guess it must be. Yes.

ESME 2 Yes. That's what you said. [*She moves some things off the table.*] You said they ended up in soggy balls on your tongue.

[*Lights fade.*]

Scene Two

Bedroom. ESME *is still at her typewriter.*

ESME A journal, that's it. I'll have myself keep a journal in common with all good lady writers since the beginning of time. I'll have nothing to write in it except that time passes. It's a private journal, not meant for ...

Scene Two B

P.W.P. The kitchen. COLIN 2 *is holding the phone.*

COLIN 2 Barbara – is that you? Yes ... she's started to keep a journal. What? No, nothing interesting, not yet ... just a lot of talk about mountains ...
[ESME 2 *enters deliberately, loudly.* COLIN 2 *puts phone down, flustered.*]

ESME 2 Have a good day?

COLIN 2 Tidied a few things up. Yourself? Go out?

ESME 2 You know I didn't go out.

COLIN 2 I'll mow the lawn on the weekend.

ESME 2 Yes? [*Starts to stack dishes.*]

COLIN 2 Then you can take a chair outside. Read a book maybe.

ESME 2 Hm.

COLIN 2 Well then the newspaper, that doesn't take much concentration. Did the boy deliver the paper? We ran that feature I wrote last month. Food pricing policies in Poland –

ESME 2 My glasses are upstairs.

COLIN 2 Well you don't have to read it. I doubt if anyone else will 'round here.

ESME 2 What are you staring at?

COLIN 2 Nothing. Nothing ... just looking. Why have you turned that picture round?

ESME 2 It was bothering me. It was staring.

COLIN 2 I don't care for the back.

185

ESME 2 I'll take it down.

COLIN 2 I suppose brown paper doesn't stare?

ESME 2 I'll take it down now. [*Doesn't move.*] Would you like it on your desk at the office?

COLIN 2 I'm a newspaper editor, Esme, I'm not a goddamned family doctor.

ESME 2 Matthew called.

COLIN 2 Oh? How is he?

ESME 2 I don't know. He sounded ... strange.

COLIN 2 Most three year olds sound strange on the phone.

ESME 2 I think I'll ask Barbara to bring him home.

COLIN 2 Don't do that. You'll freak again.

ESME 2 I won't. I'll do better this time.

COLIN 2 You can't confine a child to the house. You have to take him out occasionally. Are you up to that?

ESME 2 I could try.

COLIN 2 Give it another month. Leave him with Barbara. He's happy there with her kids. He hasn't exactly been screeching to come home.

ESME 2 I was thinking we could turn the living room into a playground. You know. Get a slide maybe ... we could put a swing up. Screw it into ...

COLIN 2 The ceiling won't support it.

ESME 2 A sandbox.

COLIN 2 I don't want to come home to ... I don't want to eat my supper in a sandbox.

ESME 2 If we had him back ...

COLIN 2 If we had him back you'd be beating up on him inside a week.

ESME 2 But it ...

COLIN 2 [*Firm.*] That's the end of it, Esme. He stays with your sister. I'm going to read the paper – [*Gets up. Softens, sits.*] So, what did you do today?

ESME 2 I listened to the radio.

COLIN 2 And ...?

ESME 2 I heard a talk-back show and I heard the news.

COLIN 2 And ...?

ESME 2 And? Somebody held up a bank. I forget where. I was thinking Col ... [*Pause.*] Where would you buy a gun? Col ... where would you buy a gun?

COLIN 2 I'm going into the den.

ESME 2 The den? I'll give Barbara a call and find out if she knows.

COLIN 2 How many times did you call her already? You can't keep calling her. She gets fed up with it. She's threatened to move out. She'll take an unlisted number, then what?

ESME 2 She wouldn't.

COLIN 2 We don't want to get on the wrong side of Barbara. Why don't you call someone else if you must keep using the phone.

ESME 2 There's no one else to call. You won't let me call you. They won't even put me through on your switchboard.

COLIN 2 Jesus! D'you know what it's like working on a newspaper? Phones going all the time!

ESME 2 Not out here. Nothing happens out here.

COLIN 2 Of course they won't put you through. They can't be loading the lines down with a dozen crank calls from you every day. Pretty soon you'll be calling me up when I'm in the next room.

ESME 2 I called the talk-back show.

COLIN 2 [Alarmed.] You didn't give your name?

ESME 2 No.

COLIN 2 Thank God for small mercies.

ESME 2 We talked about bank robberies.

COLIN 2 As long as you didn't give your name.

ESME 2 I told him about my fantasy.

COLIN 2 Which one?

ESME 2 About robbing a bank.

COLIN 2 You?

ESME 2 Yes. I want to rob a bank. To show that I can do it. To show I can still do something. There aren't many mothers who ...

COLIN 2 A female bank robber. I'd dare you to do it if I though it'd help you to get out of the house.

ESME 2 He said I'd have to disguise myself as a man if I wanted to get away with it. Then it'd lose its significance.

COLIN 2 Did you tell him about your other fantasies?

ESME 2 No.

COLIN 2 And did you tell him you daren't leave your kitchen?

187

That your sister has to buy our groceries and look after our child? Did you ask him how in the world anyone could rob a bank while they're sitting at the kitchen table suffering from agoraphobia?

ESME 2 I don't *suffer* from agoraphobia.

COLIN 2 Then what is wrong with you?

ESME 2 Nothing. There's nothing the matter with me.

COLIN 2 Okay. Go upstairs then.

ESME 2 No. No ... I don't want to. The faucet on the bath's dripping.

COLIN 2 I told you last week. Call a plumber.

ESME 2 It only needs a washer.

COLIN 2 Well fix it yourself. I'm not up to it. It'll cost twice as much if I tackle it.

ESME 2 The hot water bill's going to be astronomical.

COLIN 2 I'll call Barbara. I'll ask her to wait here with you this once. I can't take a day off work just to sit around waiting for a damned plumber.

ESME 2 I tried to take a nap this afternoon. I couldn't get to sleep. It scared me. The eternal dripping. Chinese water torture. I'm not going upstairs again. I'll sleep down here.

COLIN 2 Okay. Okay, I'll do it. I'll change the washer on the bathroom tap. I'll change the washer.

ESME 2 You will? [*Pause.*] The moderator said it really shouldn't be necessary to leave the house. [*As she speaks* COLIN *is getting up and putting on his raincoat.*] Where are you going?

COLIN 2 Out. I'm going back to the office. I have a couple of things to check out.

ESME 2 Oh.

COLIN 2 I won't be long – okay?

ESME 2 Yes. Okay.

COLIN 2 I won't take the car. I'll leave it in the drive – you might want to get out for a while.

ESME 2 No. I don't think I will.

COLIN 2 What are you scared of? It's been so long. When's it going to end Esme? What is it?

ESME 2 [*Shrugs. Pause.*] You have to understand that it's better to stay inside.

COLIN 2 I try. Why can't you try? Try can't you?

ESME 2 I am. Every day I try. I just can't ... it must be this place. We should go back to the city. [COLIN 2 *sighs.*] I'll try harder.

COLIN 2 I'll fix the tap when I get back ... okay? Oh, and by the way, Jack MacNeil is in town next weekend. I've invited him to supper on Friday. [*Goes to door.*] Bye. [*Pause.*] I said bye.

ESME 2 Yes.

[COLIN 2 *exits.*]

Scene Two C

Bedroom. ESME *with typewriter.*

ESME I do understand. I do understand that telephones don't work on stage ... but ... just one more time. I promise I won't use it again.

Scene Two D

P.W.P. ESME 2 *in kitchen dials phone.*

ESME 2 Barbara? Barb ... it's me. He just left.

[*Lights up on* BARBARA *holding her phone.*]

BARBARA Don't panic. Don't panic baby.

ESME 2 I'm panicking aren't I?

BARBARA What did he say?

ESME 2 I can't remember ... he said ... he said he was going to the office.

BARBARA Then that's where he's gone.

ESME 2 Barbara?

BARBARA What?

ESME 2 That is you isn't it?

BARBARA Of course it's me. I've just shoe-horned Matthew into bed. He wanted to watch the Bionic Woman.

ESME 2 Who's she?

189

BARBARA   A TV lady with superhuman powers. God, life was simpler when we didn't have TV. Cities!

ESME 2   This is a city?

BARBARA   Sure feels like it to me.

ESME 2   I know he didn't go to the office. Is he meeting someone? [*Pause.*] Barb ... if I don't needle then there's silence. Silence and a dripping tap. It's always been ... abrasive ... but now it's just sandpaper on raw flesh. What if he leaves me on my own? In this godforsaken ...?

BARBARA   What are you talking about? Laugh. Jees. Where's your sense of humour? You used to be a real clown. Think back to the old days in Montreal.

ESME 2   I daren't.

BARBARA   You never took yourself too seriously ...

ESME 2   Is it because I'm visual?

BARBARA   You were a clown.

ESME 2   Yes. [*Suddenly.*] I've been thinking of robbing a bank.

BARBARA   That's more like it. [*Laughs.*]

ESME 2   D'you think it's a good idea?

BARBARA   Need an accomplice?

ESME 2   I'll surprise everyone.

BARBARA   You sure will.

ESME 2   He's inviting Jack for supper on Friday.

BARBARA   Who's Jack?

ESME 2   They used to be best buddies. [*Pause.*] He said he wasn't going to take the car tonight.

BARBARA   What?

ESME 2   He's taken it. I heard him.

BARBARA   I have to go now Es.

ESME 2   I won't call again tonight, eh?

BARBARA   Not tonight.

[BARBARA *puts the phone down.*]

ESME 2   Tomorrow? Barb ... Barb? You haven't gone have ...? Barb! [ESME 2 *puts the phone down. Walks around kitchen. Picks up newspaper. Looks at ads. Goes to phone. Dials.* [*Odd, strained voice.*] Hello? Hello ... I'm calling about your advertisement. Yes. How big is the bath tub? It's sold? Gold? No ... sold ... oh I see. No ... don't hang up. Tell me about it anyway. You see we have a leaking tap and I thought if we were to replace the

bath tub ... hello? I mean, I wonder what we missed ...
was it a bargain? No? No ... [*Puts phone down. Dials
again.*] ... 5932 ... hello. I believe you have a chesterfield
for sale. Yes. Gold and blue brocade? That sounds very ...
suitable. I mean it sounds nice, real nice ... you see my
husband seems to have taken a dislike to ours. I once
slept on it for two weeks. He won't sit on it. How many
people does it seat? [*Pause.*] Would that be big people or
little people? My husband's a fairly small man ... about
my size. He's gone out. He said he was going to the
office but I don't believe that. [*Pause.*] Three big people.
Yes. Well, we won't be needing it just yet, but maybe ...
maybe soon. If I could call you back. It was nice talking
to you. Real nice. Yes. How big is big? ... No don't go
away! ... I have a ... something I'd like to talk to you about
... I suppose you don't have a gun for sale? [*Replaces
receiver. Lights dim on her as she dials again.*]

Scene Three

P.W.P. 11:00 p.m. Lights up on COLIN 2 *and* BARBARA *in*
BARBARA'S *house.* COLIN 2 *is just replacing the receiver
on the phone.*

COLIN 2 I'd better get back. She's probably taken it off the hook.
BARBARA She could be making a bunch of calls.
COLIN 2 Who to at this time of night?
BARBARA Oh, I don't know. It could be anyone. She's lonely Colin.
Lonely. [*She opens the door for him to leave.*]
COLIN 2 Okay. I get the hint. You're a good person Barb. I can talk
to you.
BARBARA Talk?
COLIN 2 Yeah – really talk.
BARBARA Wow. That's really talking?
COLIN 2 Jesus, she's going to get out of the house. She's going to
get out if I have to drag her out.
BARBARA Just be patient.
COLIN 2 Patient! Patient! [*He roars.*]
BARBARA [*Laughing and pushing him out.*] Do it at home. You'll

191

wake the kids. Between you and that damned bird out
there ... [*Walks out onto the porch with him.*
Lights down.]

Scene Four A

Bedroom.

ESME A play? Dare I have her writing a play? Yes. What the
hell!

Scene Four B

P.W.P. Lights up briefly on ESME 2 *arranging papers on*
kitchen table. She leaves.
Lights down.

Scene Four C

P.W.P. Later. Kitchen. COLIN 2 *(alone) dials phone.*
Lights up on BARBARA *stumbling to her phone.*

COLIN 2 Barbara? Is that you? Did I get you up?

BARBARA That's okay, I only just got to bed anyway. The peacock's
in full cry tonight. It sounds mad.

COLIN 2 I haven't even thought about bed yet.

BARBARA [*Yawning.*] Lordie, it's two o'clock.

COLIN 2 I had to replace a washer.

BARBARA That's cool Colin.

COLIN 2 She's asleep. On the chesterfield in the den.

BARBARA Good. That's good.

COLIN 2 Listen – this is exciting. She's started to write again.

BARBARA The journal?

COLIN 2 No ... looks like a play. I have it right here.

BARBARA Is it good?

COLIN 2 Good?

BARBARA Does it make sense?

COLIN 2 I'm not an expert. The thing is she's writing again. She's hardly put pen to paper since the *Media Mumbles* three years ago.

BARBARA Well, why don't you let her tell you about it?

COLIN 2 D'you think this is a breakthrough?

BARBARA If she can finish it –

COLIN 2 Maybe she really is going to pull through this. Maybe we can straighten things out and then ... What do you think?

BARBARA I don't know Colin. [*Yawn.*] Why don't you go to bed?

COLIN 2 I'm sorry. Sorry love. I'm keeping you up. Next thing we know she'll be going outside the house and then ... I'm being optimistic aren't I?

BARBARA If I was optimistic I'd believe my day didn't begin at six o'clock in the morning.

COLIN 2 I'll cut the grass on the weekend.

BARBARA Colin!

COLIN 2 Oh sorry love. I'm sorry.

BARBARA That's okay.

COLIN 2 Oh and Barb ...

BARBARA What?

COLIN 2 [*Very softly.*] I love you.
[*He replaces the receiver.*]

Scene Five

Bedroom.
    ESME *is crouching over her typewriter. Phone beside bed rings. She ignores it, continues to work. Ring stops. She types. Ringing starts again. She picks up phone. Meanwhile we see* COLIN *in newsroom, dialling.*

COLIN Hi honey.

ESME What?

COLIN You okay?

ESME Oh –

COLIN No pains?

ESME No.

COLIN You okay?

ESME Oh. Oh – yes. I'm okay. Who were you just talking to?

COLIN No one. I've got the newsroom to myself for a change. Just checking in –

ESME That's cool Colin.

[*She puts the phone down absent-mindedly, wanders back to typewriter deep in thought.*

Phone rings. She lets it ring. Looks at ESME 2 *as she enters.*

Lights dim on COLIN *but should not black out.*]

Scene Six

P.W.P. A department store information booth. ESME 2 *is in outdoor clothing.*

CLERK Can I help you?

ESME 2 [*Distracted.*] What ... oh ... yes. Yes.

CLERK Yes?

ESME 2 Yes. I ... I wanted to ask you – [*Pause.*]

CLERK Excuse me ... if you could just stand aside until you've made up your mind ...

[COLIN *puts phone down. It stops ringing.*]

ESME 2 Guns. I mean ... Do they sell guns in a department store?

CLERK [*Routinely.*] Fourth floor, sporting goods – now – excuse me ...

ESME 2 Sporting? ... For sport? You see it's my husband's birthday. Do they sell small guns?

CLERK Pistols?

ESME 2 Something to fit into ... to fit in a pocket maybe.

CLERK You'll have to enquire from the sales clerk.

ESME 2 Do you need a licence?

CLERK In the sporting goods.

ESME 2 Fourth floor? You did say fourth? How do I get there?

CLERK [*Exasperated.*] Elevators to your right through menswear. [*To next customer.*] Can I help you sir?

ESME 2 Menswear? Yes. Through menswear to the elevator. [*She walks away.*] In the elevator to the fourth floor. Sporting goods. [*She exits.*]

Scene Six A

Bedroom. Phone rings. ESME *answers it.*

COLIN Listen honey –

ESME Col ... I'm ... I'm in the middle of something okay?

COLIN That's not important. [ESME *looks at receiver in silence.*] You okay? Listen, you'll call me if there's even a twinge right? Don't go through the switchboard – Rosemary takes forever.

ESME Rosemary?

COLIN I'll be stuck here for a while – I've just been in with the Big Cheese – two hours would you believe – but listen – I've persuaded him to let me do a switch – I don't have to leave tomorrow! Hear that?

ESME You don't?

COLIN Jees – I thought he was gonna fire me on the spot –

ESME That's great news Colin.

COLIN I have to spend the next 24 hours briefing my replacement, so if you can just hold out that long –

ESME So he fired you?

COLIN I didn't say that.

ESME And you don't mind?

COLIN Esme, I'm not quitting the job.

ESME But you're staying home?

COLIN Yes. Yes. [ESME *sighs, relieved.*] Es?

ESME How would I look in a white suit?

COLIN Like a fucking sugar cube!

ESME Virginal?

COLIN We're not getting married again if that's what you're ... the pains've started haven't they?

ESME No.

COLIN Listen – if Craig gets there before I make it home you'll pick up that phone right away?

ESME He's here.

COLIN What?

ESME [*Putting phone down.*] I'm such a bitch to you Colin –

COLIN Esme – are you there?

ESME [*Going back to her writing.*] That's the secret – wait. Wait until they're nearly on top of you. Wait until you can reach out and touch them. Wait until you can see the whites of their eyes.
[COLIN *begins to dial again, changes his mind, is undecided, finally picks up his outdoor coat and flings himself into it.*]

Scene Seven

P.W.P. That evening, kitchen of COLIN *and* ESME's *house,* COLIN 2 *sits at the table reading the paper.* ESME 2 *enters (not wearing outdoor clothes.)*

ESME 2 I cooked something special tonight.

COLIN 2 Why? Is it a special occasion?

ESME 2 No. Not very. Pork chops in beer.

COLIN 2 Did you use that last beer?

ESME 2 It was in the fridge.

COLIN 2 I've been thinking about that beer all the way home. Stuck in a traffic jam in a crowded bus thinking about that last bottle of beer.

ESME 2 Well you're going to have to eat it now.

COLIN 2 Why'd you have to do a special tonight anyway? You can do a special on Friday ... when Jack's with us ... oh and by the way, I invited Barbara.

ESME 2 Yes. She told me. She was here this afternoon.

COLIN 2 I know.

ESME 2 How do you know?

COLIN 2 She called me. She called me at the office.

ESME 2 How come she can call the office and I can't?

COLIN 2 Because she only calls in emergencies.

ESME 2 What emergency?

COLIN 2 She said she came here this afternoon. She came because you weren't answering the phone. And you didn't answer the door when she got here.

ESME 2 I did answer the door. I let her in.

COLIN 2 That was the second time around. She took the kids to the park and then came back.

ESME 2 Matthew didn't want to leave.

COLIN 2 She said she got the distinct impression that you'd been out. Did you go out Esme?

ESME 2 Out? You know I don't go out.

COLIN 2 You don't have to deny it. I'll be more than happy ...

ESME 2 It wasn't an emergency.

COLIN 2 No – it was good news. Not an emergency. Good news. Where did you go?

ESME 2 Nowhere.

COLIN 2 Okay ... it's your life ... you do what you like. I'm happy for you that's all. It must be hell to be caged up in the house.

ESME 2 It's not hell.

COLIN 2 I only want to help.

ESME 2 It's okay. I don't need any help. You and Barbara ... everyone wants to help. You're all crowding in on me, telling me I'm sick. I guess you've told Jack MacNeil I'm sick?

COLIN 2 Agoraphobia is a sickness. I've talked about it with several doctors. It's a perfectly treatable sickness but no one can treat you if you won't leave the house.

ESME 2 Catch 22.

COLIN 2 You should have something to occupy your mind. I don't know why you stopped writing.

ESME 2 They don't ask me for plays anymore that's why. They don't invite me to conferences. My publisher's stopped calling. Everything's going on very well without me. It's like being dead. I don't exist.

COLIN 2 You can only say no so many times Esme. After that you are dead.

ESME 2 Anyway ... I have got something to occupy my mind.

COLIN 2 [*Pause.*] Well?

ESME 2 I'm going to rob a bank.

COLIN 2 Oh Christ.

ESME 2 You don't think I can do it.

COLIN 2 I don't think you can do anything much right now.

ESME 2 It's something I want to try for myself.

COLIN 2 [*Sniffing.*] What's that? I can smell something ...

197

ESME 2 Oh. [*Giggles.*] I'm burning your beer! [*Pause.*] What were
you doing at Barbara's last night?

COLIN 2 At Barbara's?

ESME 2 Yes.

COLIN 2 What are you talking about?

ESME 2 Matthew said he saw your car in the drive.

COLIN 2 Our son's going to have a more vivid imagination than
his mother.

ESME 2 [*Rejoining him.*] He said he saw a yellow car in the drive.
He said he heard your voice. Was that imagination?

COLIN 2 I should get over there more often and visit with him.

ESME 2 I was thinking. I was thinking maybe we could have the
kid here and give Barbara a chance for a break. She
could go to Mexico.

COLIN 2 Mexico?

ESME 2 It's a long way away. [*Pause.*] Matthew has a hamster.

COLIN 2 Yes?

ESME 2 He says it's prophetic.

COLIN 2 He doesn't know the meaning of the word.

ESME 2 That's what he said though.

COLIN 2 The word's not in his vocabulary. [*Pause.*] I hope there's
nothing wrong with the kid.

ESME 2 He's okay. He just wants to come home that's all. He
keeps asking Rawguts when he can come home.
Rawguts the oracle.

COLIN 2 'Rawguts' needs a bigger cage.

ESME 2 How do you know?

COLIN 2 Barbara told me. And he calls it Fred.

ESME 2 When she phoned you at the office?

COLIN 2 Yes. When she phoned me.

ESME 2 Oh, so that was the emergency.

BLACKOUT

Scene Eight

P.W.P. Phone rings in darkness. Lights up in BARBARA's
home. BARBARA *is holding the phone.*

BARBARA Damn. Damn you Esme. Why don't you answer the phone any more? Come on. Come on baby. [*Phone continues to ring as she speaks.*] Esme, sometimes I could ... sometimes I'd like to ... You know Esme, last night I had this corny dream. I was driving a car ... a white car down the centre of the road with the two front wheels straddling the white line ... and I went over a hill, and you were standing ... you were standing in the middle of the road in a white silk suit with a white scarf ... reading a speech from one of your plays, a speech about a child, about a child, and I ...

ESME 2 [*Picking up the phone in her kitchen.*] Hello?

BARBARA I couldn't stop.

ESME 2 What?

BARBARA Oh ... oh ... hi! It's me. You weren't answering.

ESME 2 [*Cold.*] No.

BARBARA You haven't called for a couple of days. [*Silence.*] I just wanted to know if you wanted me to pick up any groceries for tomorrow night? Jack's still coming eh? Do you have a menu planned?

ESME 2 [*Cool.*] Colin can do it. It's his party.

BARBARA Do you want me to come?

ESME 2 That doesn't seem to be up to me.

BARBARA Look Esme ... what is it?

ESME 2 Nothing. Nothing at all. How's Matthew?

BARBARA He's a bit upset right now. His hamster escaped.

ESME 2 That must be a prophecy.

BARBARA What do you mean?

ESME 2 Rawguts is an oracle.

BARBARA What?

ESME 2 Matthew told me. Very softly. When no one was listening. I hear things even when people say them very softly. When they whisper them into the telephone ... Tell him not to be upset. [*She puts the phone down.*]
BLACKOUT

199

Scene Nine

P.W.P. JACK *and* COLIN 2 *at the bar of the Royal Hotel.*

JACK And I said not Ethiopia ... I told him I'd had enough of the Middle East. Beirut was the pits. Let them wipe each other out but keep me away from it. Too much responsibility – the wars are being fought with headlines these days – lead's out of fashion.

COLIN 2 There's plenty of lead in printer's ink.

JACK You were wise to pack it in Colin.

COLIN 2 Was I? I miss the highs. Even if they were vicarious.

JACK Nothing's vicarious in this game. Russ Pringle took a bullet in his butt. Did you hear that?

COLIN 2 [*Laughing.*] Yes. Poor old Russ.

JACK Long as they didn't hit his drinking arm eh? The opposition weren't too sorry when you quit. You were landing too many plums for our side. Didn't expect to find you in this backwater though. Bit of a comedown isn't it?

COLIN 2 It suits – the pay's not bad. What brings you out here?

JACK The business at Cominco.

COLIN 2 That's all?

JACK Isn't that enough?

COLIN 2 Oh sure.

JACK We've been taking some flak lately about lack of coverage out here in the west.

COLIN 2 Rightly so.

JACK So they've asked for a couple of features. Could take a while ... What kind of coverage have you given the strike?

COLIN 2 Hardly touch it. Advertisers.

JACK [*Long pause.*] You know something? I don't think I'd've recognized you.

COLIN 2 No? I got a couple of teeth capped. Union dental plan.

JACK You don't mind if I say this? I mean we used to be buddies eh? But Jesus man ... you look like a dying duck. A dead duck ... that's been hung a couple of weeks too long. Jesus, you'd pass for a bank clerk!

200

COLIN 2 I don't spend much time preening. Shall we eat? I'm sorry the arrangements got screwed up. Esme's not feeling well tonight.

JACK Not pregnant again? Last time I saw her she was bursting at the seams.

COLIN 2 No. No ... one's enough.

JACK Hasn't had any Broadway hits lately then?

COLIN 2 She hasn't written anything lately.

JACK Yes. I had heard whispers.

COLIN 2 So – how's the rugby?

JACK Folks used to take bets on how long you two'd stay together. I still get the odd gossip hound trying to tap me to find out why the perfect couple went into hiding.

COLIN 2 We didn't. We just decided to duck out while we were on top and move to a quieter situation. Lead a more healthy life.

JACK Sounds like retirement.

COLIN 2 Well you know ... life in the big city was nerve shattering. We don't have the worries out here, and Esme wanted to be nearer her sister.

JACK The glamorous sister? Didn't I meet her once?

COLIN 2 Barbara.

JACK Come on ... jog my memory.

COLIN 2 Oh she went back to the land.

JACK You should give me her address.

COLIN 2 She has two kids. You wouldn't be interested.

JACK And you are. Well ... I'm glad to see you haven't retired completely Colin.

COLIN 2 Jack ... what do you know about agoraphobia?

JACK Fear of agors.

COLIN 2 Spaces. Fear of open ...

JACK Well, there's plenty of that around here.

COLIN 2 I guess some people get off on being confined. The prison authorities are even beginning to acknowledge that aren't they?

JACK Are you saying that Esme ...?

COLIN 2 Maybe it's me too. Esme and me ... both building fences round each other. Neither of us really wanting to be here but ... You couldn't label my malady agoraphobia. More like battle fatigue.

JACK What are you saying? Shake yourself up man and get back into the swim.

COLIN 2 I don't think I could face up to the old life again. Esme probably feels the same. I don't have it in me any more. The rat race ...

JACK I don't believe you. You're always the first on the front line.

COLIN 2 They only ever sent me to the war zones. That's all I knew. That's all I wanted to know. We're defined by war ... or its absence. Isn't that right?

JACK You need a few more drinks. Blow away the cobwebs.

COLIN 2 Yeah.

JACK Come on. Let's buy a couple of bottles. Take them up to my room and order a pizza. Let's tank up and then maybe we can talk sense. That woman was always a fiend.

[*They get up from the table and exit.*]

Scene Ten

P.W.P. The kitchen of ESME's *home later the same night.* ESME 2 *sits alone at the table.*

COLIN 2 *and* JACK *enter drunkenly from darkened hallway.*

JACK [*Singing to tune of MacNamara's band.*] O ma name is Jack MacNeil and I'm the leader of the pack. I've come for Esme Creary and I want her on her back.

COLIN 2 [*Calling over* JACK.] Esme! Es ... we're back. I brought you a present, Es. Have we got any booze in the house? [*Whispers.*] Kitchen light's on. Maybe she's still up. What time is it? I seem to have lost my watch.

JACK One thirty.

COLIN 2 [*Explodes, trying to suppress laughter.*] Es. I brought Jack home. You remember? Old Jackie MacNeil? It's been a few years ... Would you believe that? Yes it's ... [*They burst into the kitchen.*]

ESME 2 Hello.

COLIN 2 What are you doing?

ESME 2 Just sitting.

COLIN 2 [*To* JACK.] She's just sitting. At the kitchen table. The lady playwright.

ESME 2 Is there a law against sitting?

COLIN 2 Yes there is. There damned well should be. It should be a privilege. Who was it stood up to write? Hemingway was it? It's a privilege for old Russ Pringle. He had his ass blown off! [*Laughs.*] We got any booze? We got any beer? Well?

ESME 2 We've got some cold pork chops.

COLIN 2 How'd you like that Jack? How's that for service? You ask your wife for a beer and she offers you a cold pork chop. Jack's gonna help you. Aren't you Jack?

JACK What?

COLIN 2 We made a bet. He bet me he could get you out of the house. Didn't you Jack?

ESME 2 You'd need a gun.

COLIN 2 Okay, so we'll get a gun!

JACK We'll get a gun! [*Laughs.*]

ESME 2 [*To* JACK.] What are you, a shadow or something?

JACK Shadow?

ESME 2 [*Mocking.*] Shadow?

COLIN 2 I want you to have a talk with old Jack.

ESME 2 Jack can't talk. He's a shadow.

JACK [*Uncomfortable.*] I don't know. I don't know Col.

ESME 2 I think I'll go to bed.

JACK Sit down. Sit down will you? [*Doubtful, tipsy.*] Won't you?

ESME 2 What for?

COLIN 2 Jack wants to talk with you.

ESME 2 You've been drinking disinfectant again.

COLIN 2 Joke. That's a private joke Jack. [*Plays with words.*] Joke Jack! [*Laughs, opens and closes cupboard doors.*]

ESME 2 What are you looking for?

COLIN 2 I'm looking for some booze. There must be some sherry. Something.

ESME 2 The disinfectant's under the sink.

COLIN 2 This? [*Takes out a bottle.*] This is disinfectant.

ESME 2 That's what I said.

COLIN 2 I'm looking for booze.

JACK So you don't like going out Esme?

ESME 2 No. No ... I like it in here. On my own. In my kitchen. I like to do things on my own. Like going to bed.

COLIN 2 Sit down!

ESME 2 Goodnight.

JACK Goodnight, Es.

ESME 2 Esme.

JACK Goodnight Esme.

COLIN 2 She says she's gonna rob a bank. Can you imagine that? She's never been in a frigging bank for months. She's never been inside a bank. What are you gonna use Es? A knife and fork ... a broom? A feather duster? Stick em up! If you wanna know how to hold up a bank you should talk with Jack and me. We've looked down more gun barrels than you've had ... More gun barrels than what Jack? Go on finish it off. I've lost the knack for the fast phrase, the fast, meaningless phrase. I've been out of the game too long.

ESME 2 Goodnight.

JACK Don't go to bed.

[ESME *exits.*]

JACK I told you I'd be no help Col. I told you I'd be ...

COLIN 2 You were a help Jack. A big help. You know what I like about you? I can talk to you.

Scene Ten B

Bedroom.

ESME [*In bed. Calls.*] Colin! Col! ... [*House is empty. She moves from bed, puts typewriter aside. Sits in chair as next scene is played on bed in front of her.*]

Scene Eleven A

P.W.P. Bedroom. ESME *sits aside, watching* ESME 2 *and* COLIN 2. *(Following morning.)*

Scene Eleven A

ESME 2 [*Sitting on edge of the bed watching* COLIN.] Colin!
[COLIN 2 *groans.*] It's eleven o'clock. [COLIN 2 *groans.*]
They've been calling.

COLIN 2 Tell them I'm sick.

ESME 2 You have to go. It's only a hangover.

COLIN 2 I'm sick.

ESME 2 You've got to go to the office.

COLIN 2 It's Saturday. No right-minded person works on a
Saturday. Tell them I'm dead.

ESME 2 Please. Col. Oh Colin. Don't go to sleep! I can't call them.
They won't put me through.

COLIN 2 I don't think I want to go to work again. Ever. [*Gentle
snore.*]

ESME 2 Okay. So be it. So be it. [ESME 2 *gets up.* COLIN 2 *pulls the
sheets over his head.* ESME 2 *takes some of his clothes
out of the closet. Looks at them. Rejects them. Picks up
the crumpled clothes he was wearing the night before.
Slowly takes off her own clothes. Exits down stairs,
brushing past* ESME.]
BLACKOUT

Scene Eleven B

P.W.P. Bedroom. ESME 2 *and* COLIN 2. *Later that day.
Lights up.* ESME 2 *sits on the bed, as before, dressed in
her own clothes.*

ESME 2 Feeling better?

COLIN 2 No. How long does it take to get over a hangover
anyway? I'm out of practice.

ESME 2 I told them you were sick. I don't think they believed
me. I called six times before they'd put me through.
They're well trained. Even on Saturday.

COLIN 2 Everyone gets sick on a Saturday morning. It's because it
follows Friday night.

ESME 2 Do they all stay in bed till Saturday night?

COLIN 2 Don't bitch at me. Not tonight.

ESME 2 Well the paper still came out. You're not indispensible.

COLIN 2 Where is it?

ESME 2 I used it to fan the fire.

COLIN 2 Don't tell me you burned it. Good God, can't I trust you even with that?

ESME 2 I didn't say I burned it.

COLIN 2 Well?

ESME 2 It got burned.

COLIN 2 Jesus! [*Gets up.*] What's this then? What's this? [*He picks up the paper.*] Jees ... another bank robbery? They've got to be low on copy.

ESME 2 It was a small one.

COLIN 2 The size is irrelevant. It's boring. It's ...

ESME 2 It's Saturday. It was a credit union. The banks are closed.

COLIN 2 Repetitive. It's repetitive. Look at this. This headline's three times too long. 'Lone gunman escapes with $10,000 in yellow hatchback.' Well what difference does the car make? Who cares?

ESME 2 The owner of the car?

COLIN 2 Ach! [*Puts paper aside.*] Did Jack call?

ESME 2 I don't know.

COLIN 2 What d'you mean you don't know?

ESME 2 I wasn't answering the phone. Not today.

COLIN 2 Oh for God's sake. Haven't you made that thing up with Barbara yet? [*No reply.*] We can't afford to quarrel with Barbara. [*Sighs.*]

ESME 2 Then you'd better go over there and tell her.

COLIN 2 I've got a headache Esme. Why don't we just sit here in silence for a while? Why don't we try sitting in silence for a week?

BLACKOUT

Scene Twelve

COLIN *and* ESME*'s house.*

COLIN [*Entering through front door, calls up.*] You okay? I grabbed a quick coffee break, jumped in a cab. – [*Looks around.*] Well, where are they? [*Goes upstairs.*]

Scene Twelve

[ESME *is in bed with typewriter. She looks up.*]

COLIN Craig – Jack. What's her name – [*Takes typewriter away from bed.*]

ESME You don't remember her name?

COLIN Barb. Oh come on Es, I haven't got time for games. I told you the situation at work –

ESME At work.

COLIN They're on the patio! [*Begins to go downstairs. Stops. Realizes. Turns and goes slowly back to bedroom.*] We're gonna talk.

ESME Now?

COLIN Now.

ESME But you have to get back to work.

COLIN I want some answers. First. That boy. What's it gonna do to you bringing that boy here – *if* that's what you're doing – are you really off your head? [ESME *shrugs.*] Don't smart-ass me Esme.

ESME He's here now.

COLIN Here?

ESME In this room. [*Rubs her stomach.*]

COLIN [*Looks at her. Pause.*] It was just a ploy huh? And I fell for it – just a ploy to keep me from leaving town –

ESME No.

COLIN [*Grabs her.*] Es!

ESME Please go away – I have to work –

COLIN You have me like a puppet! You think my work's not important right? That Sudan thing – let me tell you – listen – you wanna know why I didn't tell you? I wanted to protect you! I mean ... [*Fishes for a better word.*] *protect* you – you think that's funny right?

ESME I'm not laughing.

COLIN You ... you're suffocating me, you know that? Years, years I've spent trying to be ... I dunno, trying to be some kind of – Rhett Butler to please you – don't laugh!

ESME [*Overlapping.*] Frankly darling I don't give a damn! Sorry, I couldn't resist ...

COLIN [*Overlapping.*] So what *am* I supposed to be. Some androgynous flunky? Is that it? Yes ma'am, no ma'am, may I borrow your panties ma'am! Why don't you make up your mind what you want?

207

ESME I want you.

COLIN And I don't want to blurr the edge any more ... I have to work dammit. It's women who have kids, not men. And why do you have to make me sound like a walking cliché ...? [*Puts his head in his hands.* ESME *looks over him to where next scene is already starting.*]

Scene Thirteen

P.W.P. COLIN 2 *and* BARBARA *in* BARBARA*'s house. Lights up on* BARBARA, *transformed; no longer frowsy, she looks glamorous. She is applying the finishing touches to her make-up when* COLIN 2 *enters.*

COLIN 2 Well ... here I am. Seven o'clock on the dot, just as ordered. Your friendly baby sitter. Matter of fact it'll be good to spend an hour with my son. I haven't seen him for a while have I?

BARBARA No. No ... he's been asking for you.

COLIN 2 I'm a lousy father, isn't that right? Tell me I'm a lousy father. I'm a lousy everything else. Haven't spoken a word to my wife for nearly a week.

BARBARA [*Lightly.*] Don't let it depress you.

COLIN 2 Where are you off to then? All dressed up ... you look stunning Barb. Almost as good as that damned bird in your yard. Hey ... make sure you come back early eh?

BARBARA I'm a bit late. D'you mind if I borrow the car?

COLIN 2 I walked over. I've been trying to leave it at home more ... give her a bit of an incentive to get out of the house. I think it's working. I'll swear she's used half a tank of gas. Maybe she's improving Barb. Maybe we'll turn the corner yet.

BARBARA Good.

COLIN 2 You two aren't on speaking terms yet?

BARBARA No. She knows that you were here last week. She knows, Colin. I told you what that'd do.

COLIN 2 She doesn't know anything. And even if she did ... well she's got nothing to fear has she? Ach, why don't you just make one more effort with her?

208

Scene Thirteen

BARBARA I think I was probably doing too much for her anyway.

COLIN 2 What do you mean?

BARBARA Shielding her. Jack says I should let her be more independent. I mean if she had to look after Matthew and get out to the supermarket ...

COLIN 2 Jack?

BARBARA Yes.

COLIN 2 You mean ... But ... he found you?

BARBARA He told me you wouldn't give him the address.

COLIN 2 That wouldn't stop him. Damned newspaperman. Is that where you're going now? Are you going to meet him?

BARBARA Yes ... I am as a matter of fact. Do I have to have your permission? You were going to introduce us anyway.

COLIN 2 You'd better go then hadn't you? You don't want to keep Jack MacNeil waiting. You'd better go.

BARBARA Are you sure you'll be okay? You just have to put the kids to bed.

COLIN 2 Oh yes. Yes. What's on TV?

BARBARA See you Colin.

COLIN 2 Yes. Have a good time. He's a married man you know ... always the lady killer. Never could keep his hands off ... even in Saigon when he knew half of them were poxy ... [BARBARA *touches his shoulder lightly, then exits.* COLIN *continues as if she were still there.*] At least I assume he's not divorced yet. Always a ladies' man ... always. You have to be careful, young Barbara. You have to watch your step. I'm telling you this for your own good. Nobody's safe when he's around ... double-dealing bum ..

CHILD'S VOICE [*Offstage.*] Dad! Dad!

COLIN 2 No. I didn't mean you Matthew. Your Auntie Barbara's gone out on the town. Let's see what we can do to entertain ourselves. [*Goes over and looks at hamster cage. Turns the wheel.*]

CHILD'S VOICE Daddy! [COLIN 2 *looks over to where voice is coming from but doesn't move.*]

BLACKOUT

Scene Fourteen

ESME *picks up doll and hugs it, goes and sits on stairs.*
Looks down and sees ESME 2 *at bottom of stairs, a dim,*
shadowy figure in a white silk suit.

Scene Fourteen A

P.W.P. Early morning, dim light. COLIN 2 *is in bed.* ESME 2
brushes past ESME *and goes up to bedroom. She dumps*
a pile of boxes on the bed, is about to exit when COLIN's
voice halts her.

COLIN 2 [*Sleepy.*] What's going on ... what's happening?

ESME 2 I'm moving my things back upstairs. [*Pause.*] Are you
awake? I'm tired of the chesterfield.

COLIN 2 No.

ESME 2 You're always sleeping.

COLIN 2 It's early Esme. Let me sleep will you? It's been a grim
week. Two guys off with 'flu ... What's going on? What's
that you're wearing?

ESME 2 Like it?

COLIN 2 What the ...?

ESME 2 Silk.

COLIN 2 Where did you get it?

ESME 2 Bought it.

COLIN 2 *You* bought it?

ESME 2 Yup. Went shopping yesterday. Got a whole slew of new
things ... a coat, shoes, this suit ...

COLIN 2 You ...?

ESME 2 Summer is a comin' in ... Like it?

COLIN 2 Very virginal. The white virgin breaks the ice. Twelve
days of silence!

ESME 2 Thirteen. Barb picked it out. I was tired of wearing your
clothes.

210

COLIN 2 Mine? When did you ever ... What did you use for money?

ESME 2 Oh ... I have money. Well? How do I look?

COLIN 2 You could use (lose) some (more) weight. [*Depending on actress.*]

ESME 2 I'll work on it.

COLIN 2 Can't we discuss this transformation later? Breakfast time for instance?

ESME 2 I wasn't going to let Barb leave me behind.

COLIN 2 You're trying to tell me that you've been out of the house? Is that it? Well it had to come ... I knew it had to come. I suspected you'd done it anyway.

ESME 2 You did? What did you suspect?

COLIN 2 I'm glad you got around to telling me. You certainly choose your times.

ESME 2 Do I? [*Pause.*] I think we should talk. I'm better now. Matthew's coming home.

COLIN 2 Oh no. No ... I'm not falling for that. The instant recovery. Come off it Esme. You've tried that one before. Try some other ploy, I've given up believing in miracles.

ESME 2 He'll have to come back. There's nowhere else for him to go. Come on, do get up. You're always in bed these days. You spend all your time in bed. You come home from work and you go to bed. You get up and you go to work and then you ...

COLIN 2 He stays with Barbara.

ESME 2 Barbara's going East. Montreal. With Jack. She's leaving her kids with her mother-in-law. We can't expect her mother-in-law to take ours as well.

COLIN 2 For a holiday? She's going for a ...?

ESME 2 I don't know.

COLIN 2 When did she tell you this?

ESME 2 Yesterday. Get up. It's going to be a nice day. We could go for a drive.

COLIN 2 Why didn't she tell me?

ESME 2 Why should she? She's my sister. I think we should get a new car. Something with a bit more zip in it. [*Pause.*] Besides, you're jealous of Jack aren't you? Get up. [COLIN 2 *groans.*] I put a dent in our old car.

COLIN 2 [*Groans.*] I'm not getting up.

ESME 2 I left it off at an auto body shop. They're going to repaint it. Red. I told them they were your instructions.

COLIN 2 I don't want a red car. But thanks. Thanks for telling me anyway. At 5:30 in the morning.

ESME 2 We're invited to supper at Barb's. They're leaving later tonight. Jack MacNeil'll be there. You remember Jack. We have to pick Matthew up. I just have to move this stuff ... [ESME *brings more boxes into the bedroom and dumps them.*] Oh come on Colin. Get up. [COLIN 2 *groans and disappears under the bedclothes.* ESME 2 *throws back the bedclothes, laughs playfully,* COLIN 2 *snatches them.*]

COLIN 2 Give me those.

ESME 2 Get up! [ESME 2 *disappears and humps some more boxes into the room.*]

COLIN 2 Oh move that stuff later whatever it is.

ESME 2 It's dawn. 'Look where the dawn in russet mantle clad ...' Hamlet.

COLIN 2 *See* where the dawn ... *See* ...

ESME 2 I'm the visual one, not you. [*She undoes her bag and takes a gun out, very casually.*]

COLIN 2 What's that you've got?

ESME 2 Can't you see it?

COLIN 2 It looks like a ... put the light on!

ESME 2 Well ... you'd hear it if I pulled the trigger. Maybe I should.

COLIN 2 A gun? Es ... don't point that thing at me

ESME 2 It's all right. I haven't assembled it. It's great isn't it? Feel the weight.

COLIN 2 N-n-n-n-no.

ESME 2 It's light. It's called a survivor's gun. It floats in water. It's the only one that you can get that takes to pieces like this. It's really easy to assemble ... see ... and it fits nicely into a bag. [*She begins to assemble the gun.*]

COLIN 2 Give that to me.

ESME 2 I can't if you wont' get up.

COLIN 2 Esme! [*Pause.*] Esme stop that. I don't need a demonstration.

ESME 2   You need a licence for a revolver ... or any small gun ...
Did you know that?

COLIN 2   Es ...

ESME 2   Any gun that can be easily hidden. But not this one.
This ... It's semi-automatic ... look.

COLIN 2   Keep it awa ...

ESME 2   Of course. You've looked down too many gun barrels.

COLIN 2   Don't wave it around like that. Joke over. It makes me
nervous. Where'd you get it?

ESME 2   Somewhere.

COLIN 2   From Jack? Jack wouldn't be so ... put it down Esme.

ESME 2   [*Commands.*] Stay where you are.

COLIN 2   No look ...

ESME 2   Put your hands up. [*Pause.*] I got it from a department
store.

COLIN 2   You ...?

ESME 2   Ages ago. I said hands up. Now. Get out of bed.

COLIN 2   But ...

ESME 2   Up! [COLIN 2 *obeys.*] Go over to the window. Open it. Go
on. Open it. I said open the window Colin. [COLIN 2
obeys.] Say after me: 'Look where the dawn in russet
mantle clad, creeps ...'

COLIN 2   'See where the ...'

ESME 2   Look ... [*She prods him.*]

COLIN 2   [*Turning suddenly.*] Give me that thing. Give me that ...
[*Jumps her, wrestles her briefly. The gun falls.*]

ESME 2   There. It's yours.

COLIN 2   You're crazy. You're right off your head.

ESME 2   You can keep it. I don't want it any more. Oh ... do be
careful. It's loaded. I just wanted you to unstick yourself
from that mattress and take a look at the dawn ... oh
don't go back to bed.

COLIN 2   [*Gets into bed. Puts gun under pillow.*] I'm going to keep
this with me.

ESME 2   You're welcome. Colin. Col ... Come out from the
blankets! Col! [*Sighs.*] I've been writing a play Col. I've
almost finished it in the last two weeks. It's amazing
how ... I knew I could do it and I did Colin. [*Pause.*] I'm
going to have to pull myself together aren't I? Now that

we won't even have Barbara. We'll only have each other. Barbara's going back to Montreal. [*Pause.*] I wish you'd look in the drawers. [*Pause.*] I wish you'd look in the closet. [*Pause.*] Colin ... the ceiling's started to come down in the living room. Where the bathroom flooded. When you fixed the faucet, remember? It doesn't matter. It really doesn't matter ... I can live with it. I can always step over the ceiling, or I can go and sit in the yard. When you've cut the grass. I'll sit out there with a book when I'm not writing. With a book. And I'll shut Matthew in the cellar so he won't get in the way. Colin. Put that gun away. Col. ... Col! [*She screams.*]

COLIN 2 [*Aims the gun and fires. An empty click.* COLIN 2 *collapses like an empty sack.*] You bitch! I nearly ...

ESME 2 [*Laughs.*] Of course it wasn't loaded.

COLIN 2 [*Near to tears.*] I would've ...

ESME 2 It couldn't have been loaded. You watched me assemble it. I didn't have time to load it.

COLIN 2 Get out of here. Get out Esme. That's it. Go!

ESME 2 [*Laughs.*] Go?

COLIN 2 Yes. Go. Go.

ESME 2 All right. So be it. [*Laughs.*] So be it. [*Exits.*]
BLACKOUT

Scene Fourteen B

Sound of a child's voice singing: 'Humpty Dumpty sat on a wall. Humpty Dumpy had a great fall ...' Lights up. ESME *is discovered near tape deck. She stops tape. Walks over to stairs.*]

Scene Fifteen

P.W.P. Semi-dark. ESME *and* COLIN's *house. Sound of phone ringing. It rings and rings. Unanswered. Stops. Rings again.*

Sound of polite knocking on outside door.
Unanswered. Doorbell rings. Unanswered. Pause.
   Lights up on COLIN 2. *He has been in bed for several*
days, dishevelled. A row of dirty cups and glasses is
ranked against the bed. Bed is strewn with debris that
ESME 2 *left behind. Typewriter on bed.*
   Banging on outside door increased in pitch. Door is
broken in. COLIN 2 *gropes for gun which is under his*
pillow.

POLICEMAN 1 Okay. You take downstairs ... I'll go up. Take it easy eh?
   [*Brushes past* ESME, *not seeing her.* POLICEMAN 2 (CRAIG)
   searches downstairs.]
POLICEMAN 1 [*Bursting into room, gun pointed at* COLIN 2.] Police!
   COLIN 2 Eh? [POLICEMAN 1 *relaxes his guard with the gun.*] How'd
   you get in? [*Pause.*] I'm in bed.
POLICEMAN 1 Colin Creary? Put your hands up. [COLIN 2 *obeys.*
   POLICEMAN 1 *looks 'round room.*]
   COLIN 2 What day is it?
POLICEMAN 1 You've been absent from your office for several days.
   COLIN 2 So what? What the hell are you doing in my bedr ...?
POLICEMAN 1 Get up.
   COLIN 2 Get out of here. What business is it of ...?
POLICEMAN 1 We have a search warrant. [*Calls down.*] MacNeil! He's
   up here ... alive. Are you the owner of a vehicle, licence
   number PMB 083?
   COLIN 2 Why?
POLICEMAN 1 Left in Karey's autobody shop last Saturday? [*Pause.*]
   You won't object to us taking a look around. Routine.
   [*Pulls back covers revealing* COLIN 2 *curled up foetus like*
   around gun.] That gun for instance.
   COLIN 2 It's not mine.
   [POLICEMAN 2 *enters and begins search.*]
POLICEMAN 1 No. No ... would you mind if I ...?
   COLIN 2 I'm holding it for ... for someone.
   [POLICEMAN 1 *takes gun.* POLICEMAN 2 *begins to open*
   drawers, throws out wads of money. Opens boxes and
   bags, they are full of money. COLIN 2 *sinks down under*
   sheets. POLICEMAN 1 *pulls* COLIN 2 *out of bed.*]

POLICEMAN 1 Get dressed.

COLIN 2 I ...

POLICEMAN 1 Move! [COLIN 2 *picks up his pants.*]. I said move it. Move! Here! [*Thrusts shirt at him.*] Think we've got all day?

COLIN 2 I've been in bed.

POLICEMAN 1 He's been in bed!

COLIN 2 For days.

POLICEMAN 1 He's been in bed for days. Move it!

[*He pushes* COLIN 2 *downstairs past* ESME *and out of the door.* ESME *goes slowly upstairs, confronts* POLICEMAN 2 *who is just leaving; he doesn't seem to see her. He exits. She begins to tidy away the mess of papers and money. Sits on the bed looking down on the jail.*]

Scene Sixteen

P.W.P. CRAIG *and* COLIN 2 *in jail.*

[CRAIG *pushes* COLIN 2 *into jail with gun in his ribs. Tears off* COLIN 2*'s shirt. Pistol whips him. Takes shirt, feels in pockets. Tosses it aside. Does same with* COLIN 2*'s jacket.*]

COLIN 2 I'd like to make a call.

CRAIG Pants.

COLIN 2 Well, it's my right isn't it? One call?

CRAIG I said pants.

COLIN 2 What the ...?

CRAIG Off! [COLIN 2 *doesn't move.* CRAIG *walks over and feels in the pockets of his pants.* COLIN 2 *pushes him away.*]

COLIN 2 What are you? Some kind of animal? [*Unzips pants and allows them to fall without stepping out of them.*]

CRAIG On your knees.

COLIN 2 What?

CRAIG Deaf?

COLIN 2 What are you some kind of ... brute? Idiot brute? [CRAIG *pistol whips him. Forces him to step out of his pants.* COLIN 2 *goes down in his knees.*] This isn't happening.

CRAIG Think you're so big? Drop those underpants. [COLIN 2 *refuses.*] Drop!

216

COLIN 2 Look – I don't understand.

CRAIG What's to understand? Drop!

COLIN 2 I want to see a lawyer. [CRAIG *laughs*.] You won't get away with this. I'll sue ... I want to see a lawyer. Now. It's my right. My right! [CRAIG *forces him onto all fours with his gun.* COLIN 2 *gets back into a kneeling position.*] There are no charges ... what can they charge me with? Bank robbery? That's absurd. Attempted murder? I wouldn't hurt a fly. I love my wife. We play games that's all. Games ... [CRAIG *kicks him back to all fours.*] Craig ...!

CRAIG Mister MacNeil. Say it. [*Kicks.*]

COLIN 2 Mister ... Fucking mister! Mister punk, who the hell do you think you ... [CRAIG *tears off his underpants.*] I'm clean. Clean! Listen I'm sorry. I didn't mean ... I'm clean.

CRAIG I can see. I got eyes.

COLIN 2 I haven't done drugs for ...

CRAIG Been sleeping for ten days have you?

COLIN 2 I'm a journalist.

CRAIG Been snowing for ten days has it? [*Turns* COLIN 2 *around so that he is on all fours and* CRAIG *is looking at his rear. Jabs his rear with gun.*] Snowbrain. Who do you think you are anyway? Pierre fucking Trudeau? [*Kicks him.*] Who do you think you're bigger than?

COLIN 2 [*Whimpering.*] I wanna call my wife.

CRAIG Wife? Oh, it's his wife he needs.

COLIN 2 In Montreal. That's where she probably is. With her sister. I'll pay for the call. [CRAIG *jabs him viciously.* COLIN 2 *spins around, wrestles with him briefly. The gun goes off.*] BLACKOUT

Scene Seventeen

Lights come up slowly on COLIN *on patio, sitting by hammock, pushing it gently. Gets up. Tiptoes into kitchen. Gets tray with orange juice and glasses. Goes back out to hammock. Picks up baby, tries to figure out how to carry tray and baby. Finally settles on baby alone.*

Puts tray down. Tiptoes upstairs, sees that ESME *is sleeping. Puts baby to sleep in cradle (in alcove offstage). Is about to go down for orange juice when* ESME *opens one eye. He goes over, kneels by the bed, puts his head on her stomach.*

ESME [*Soothing him.*] Valderee, valderaa, valderee, valder ...

COLIN ... a hahahahaha ha! [*They clown, laugh, hug.*
Doorbell sounds. They stiffen. COLIN *gets up tentatively, goes downstairs, kicks over glasses. Ignores them, changes his mind, picks up tray and takes it into kitchen. Door bell.*]

ESME Colin!

[COLIN *opens door and ushers* JACK *and* BARBARA *in. They have aged. We see them as they are in 'real life,' an average suburban couple.* JACK *is blustery,* BARBARA *overawed.* JACK *has two bottles of champagne.* COLIN *looks out beyond them, to street.*]

JACK He's down there parking the car. Is it all meters?

COLIN Tell him I'll pay the ticket.

JACK Ach!

BARBARA Maybe we shoulda waited for him.

COLIN No, come on in. [*Hesitates, then shakes hands with* JACK, *pecks* BARB *on cheek.*]

JACK Sorry we're behind schedule.

BARBARA That clutch's been acting up ever since we left ... Is she all right?

COLIN Fine. Fine – sick of being in bed –

JACK She's antsy?

COLIN Not any more.

JACK She was like a time bomb last time. We had two false alarms – that's why I insisted on a hospital.

COLIN We wanted to do it the natural way. Glad you made it –

JACK Still chasing ambulances?

COLIN Let me get some glasses – [*While* COLIN *puts more glasses on tray,* BARBARA *and* JACK *take their coats off, look around curiously.*]

BARBARA Hey Jack, come and look at the patio. Look – a hammock. [*To* COLIN.] All we have on our porch is dogshit and kids' fire trucks –

COLIN [*Laughs.*] Come on up and say hi.
[*JACK and* BARBARA *follow him upstairs.* BARBARA *kisses* ESME, JACK *takes her hand.*]

JACK So?

BARBARA How are you?

ESME Empty.

BARBARA [*Nervous.*] I know how you feel – like an overripe cheese in the plastic bag eh? I was the same with our two. I was 3 weeks late with Iain. Isn't that how I said I felt Hon? [*Turns to* JACK, ESME *puts her knees down, and* BARBARA *sees that she is no longer pregnant.*] Oh! Es! [*Hugs her.*]

ESME Sssh! [*Indicates that baby is in next room.*]

BARBARA Boy or girl?

ESME Girl.

BARBARA What's her name?

JACK Congratulations. [*Shakes* COLIN's *hand. To* BARBARA.] I told you not to get cigars! [*Kisses* ESME, *embarrassed, still holding champagne.* COLIN *is still holding orange juice.*]

ESME No cigars?

BARBARA So what is her name?

ESME Cassandra.
[*COLIN turns sharply.*]

BARBARA Nice. Kinda old fashioned.

ESME Sandra for short –

BARBARA [*Laughs.*] Oh that's better.

COLIN [*Putting down tray casually.*] Well, isn't this civilized? The old gang together again after what ...?

JACK Years.

COLIN So much water under the ...

ESME How many bridges do you have Jack? [*Bares her teeth.*] I imagined you with less hair.

JACK Tempus bloody well fugits. [*Pause.*]

ESME No peacock shit?

BARBARA What?

ESME On your porch?

BARBARA Peacocks?

ESME That's a relief. [BARBARA *and* JACK *exchange glances.* COLIN *has walked over to the window.*]

219

ESME [*To* COLIN's *back.*] He's parking the car. [*To* BARBARA.] Where are your kids?

BARBARA We left them with my sister back home. We needed a break from them, eh Jack?

COLIN Why don't you get up for a while Es? We could go and sit on the patio. Have a few pre-prandial nibblies. She was born the night before last, and we were back here the next day. She was down in the kitchen this morning making this fantastic paté, can you believe that? 42 years old!

ESME I had to do something with the placenta.
[BARBARA *and* JACK *react to this,* COLIN *has turned back to the window, chuckling.*]

COLIN There he is! [*Spies* CRAIG *in street.*]

ESME [*Mocking.*] Pre-prandial nibblies! That's for your benefit Jack!

JACK Ach – with three kids around you learn to talk in monosyllables, eh love? [*Squeezes* BARBARA.
Doorbell sounds. JACK *goes down to let* CRAIG *in. Pauses with him by the outside door.* CRAIG *has luggage. Doesn't seem too eager to go upstairs.*]

COLIN Well – you're still looking good Barb. [*Bustles.*]

ESME What are you doing?

COLIN Tidying up.

BARBARA [*Uneasy.*] Jack was so keen to visit but I ...

COLIN Oh come on. I can pay you a compliment after 20 years!

BARBARA It's the first break he's taken since he got the agency started.

ESME Agency?

BARBARA Real estate and insurance – it's going good.

ESME I knew it!

COLIN So he's given up on newsprint?

BARBARA Ages ago – [*To* ESME.] Jack and I got out your old wedding pictures before we left. Me with my matron of honour smile and mumps ... [*Blows out her cheeks, giggles.*]

COLIN That's right. I wouldn't kiss you. It's supposed to make men sterile.

BARBARA Kissing?

COLIN Mumps, silly.

Scene Seventeen

BARBARA And I refused to shave my armpits. Heavens, the sixties!

ESME That's right, you did have mumps.

[CRAIG *bursts into the room, he is well dressed in contrast to previous scenes.*]

CRAIG Dad said ... [*He stops. Stares at* ESME. *She freezes.*]

COLIN Hey! [*Punches* CRAIG, *friendly.*] Take a look at these shoulders, Es. Where'd he get them?

[ESME *hugs her shoulders.*]

JACK [*Entering.*] All the better to tackle me with eh Craig? [*He crouches in mock rugby tackle.*]

COLIN [*To* JACK.] Still playing the old game?

JACK Not me.

COLIN I joined the over 40's club! [*To* CRAIG.] You?

JACK Ach – it's all hockey in our town – [*They laugh.*] Hey Craigie. This is Colin. Best man when I married your mother. Then we changed partners eh? [*Pats* ESME.] Very civilized. [*During this* ESME *is staring at* CRAIG.]

COLIN [*To* CRAIG.] So ... are you in college?

JACK Sure is – tell them what you're studying Craig. [*To* ESME.] This'll get to you!

ESME What.

CRAIG Creative writing.

COLIN You study that?

ESME You're not in the police?

CRAIG What?

[*Pause.*]

ESME Your picture doesn't do you justice.

COLIN Come on, let's drink this on the patio. [*Picks up champagne.*] Bit warm but what the hell. Come on Craig. Last time I saw you I coulda picked you up with one hand. Creative writing? [*To* ESME.] Bring her down. [*The baby.*]

[CRAIG *and* COLIN *exit,* COLIN *gives* CRAIG *tray to carry.* JACK *helps* ESME *out of bed.*]

ESME You go ahead. Go on. I'm not an invalid, silly –

JACK Sure? [ESME *nods.*]

BARBARA Are you breast feeding?

ESME [*Nods.*] I'm soaked.

BARBARA Oh, let's see her!

[ESME *exits to where baby is.* BARBARA *and* JACK *look at*

221

each other, he puts his arm round her and indicates that they should join CRAIG *and* COLIN.]

JACK She likes to make a grand entrance.

[COLIN *and* CRAIG *are downstairs out of earshot of the rest.*]

COLIN I shoulda been in Baghdad today.

CRAIG Our car broke down, that's why we're –

COLIN That car has more sense than I do, know that?

CRAIG What's in Baghdad?

COLIN Ali Baba for all I know! [*Laughs.*] Is there any room in that course you're taking?

CRAIG You don't need a course!

COLIN [*Shrugs.*] I need a bit of time to enjoy the peace.

CRAIG Peace?

COLIN Well, maybe it's only a cease-fire.

[JACK *and* BARBARA *join* COLIN *and* CRAIG}.]

COLIN Just talking about peace.

CRAIG He's not going to Baghdad.

JACK You're not giving it up, finally?

COLIN [*Shrugs.*] I don't think I'm up to it right now. I feel like I've been through a bit of a war and ...

JACK I wondered how much longer ... listen, they were wanting another editor on the *Gazette* back home. Chap who replaced me turned out to be a wee bit of a dud –

COLIN No offence, Jack – I'd rather take up knitting. You know –

[*Draws him aside. During this* BARBARA *is stranded on the outside.* CRAIG *goes over to stairs and stands, undecided.*]

JACK They should pension you off before you burn out.

COLIN Got a replacement part now. [*Nods upstairs. Grins.*]

JACK And then they grow up.

COLIN I watched it happen –

JACK Aye – it's quite a sight.

COLIN Done a bit of watching in our time eh? Did you ... did you ... you know ... get to hold yours?

JACK Sure – that's part of it.

COLIN It was like that time in the Sudan.

JACK What?

COLIN My knees gave way – thought I was gonna keel over.

[JACK *laughs nervously.*] I mean – see – they let me – you

222

know, hold her before they cleaned her off – it's against the rules – there was blood. [*Indicates his hands.*] And I did it. She's mine. [*Laughs.*] C'mon, let's celebrate ... [*They go through to patio. Calls.*] C'mon Es.
[*Voices only, we see their shadowy shapes, but they should not pull focus from* ESME, *hardly more than a murmur.*]

COLIN One at a time –

JACK Oh go on, open them both.

BARBARA It's the best. We bought the best –

COLIN Yea, I can see ... whoops –

BARBARA Oh, d'you have a cloth?

JACK It's all right, they'll clean ...

BARBARA [*Laughs.*] Cassandra – who was it was called that?

JACK She's dead.

BARBARA Oh Jack!

[*Meanwhile* CRAIG *goes slowly upstairs. He stands, looking at* ESME. *Long pause.* ESME *is sitting on the bed with the baby, looks over baby to* CRAIG.]

ESME Like him. Like me. You have our face. [*Indicates stomach. Laughs softly.*] It was hard as a stone. [CRAIG *approaches her slowly. She encourages him to put his hand on her stomach.*] A stone cracked open – a cave – and inside, curled up inside – life. Blind life – the wonder – the wonder of it.
[CRAIG *puts his arms round her neck. They embrace.*]
END

Margaret Hollingsworth was born in England and travelled widely, living in Italy and Japan, before becoming a Canadian citizen in 1968. Her plays have received stage productions in England and Canada and several have been aired on radio in Canada, England, West Germany, Australia and New Zealand.

Other published plays by Margaret Hollingsworth:

Alli Alli Oh.
Toronto: Playwrights Union of Canada, 1979.
This companion piece to *Islands* was first produced by Redlight Theatre, Toronto, in 1977 under the direction of Francine Volker.

Bushed. In *Operators / Bushed.*
Toronto: Playwrights Union of Canada, 1981.
First produced by the Vancouver Playhouse in 1973 under the direction of Jane Heyman and David Latham.

Mother Country.
Toronto: Playwrights Union of Canada, 1981.
First produced by Tarragon Theatre, Toronto, in 1980 under the direction of Bill Glassco.

Operators. In *Operators / Bushed.*
Toronto: Playwrights Union of Canada, 1981.
First produced by the New Play Centre, Vancouver, in 1974 under the direction of Pam Hawthorne.